YOUR PERSONAL
HOROSCOPE
2018

CANCER

D0711823

YOUR PERSONAL HOROSCOPE 2018

CANCER

22nd June–22nd July

igloobooks

igloobooks

Published in 2017
by Igloo Books Ltd
Cottage Farm
Sywell
NN6 0BJ
www.igloobooks.com

Produced for Igloo Books by Foulsham Publishing Ltd, The Old Barrel Store,
Drayman's Lane, Marlow, Bucks SL7 2FF, England

FIR003 0717
2 4 6 8 10 9 7 5 3 1
ISBN: 978-1-78670-878-6

This is an abridged version of material originally published
in Old Moore's Horoscope and Astral Diary.

Cover design by Charles Wood-Penn
Edited by Bobby Newlyn-Jones

Printed and manufactured in China

CONTENTS

1   Introduction   7

2   The Essence of Cancer:
    Exploring the Personality of Cancer the Crab   9

3   Cancer on the Cusp   15

4   Cancer and its Ascendants   17

5   The Moon and the Part it Plays in your Life   31

6   Moon Signs   35

7   Cancer in Love   39

8   Venus: The Planet of Love   43

9   Venus through the Zodiac Signs   45

10 Cancer: 2017 Diary Pages   49

11 Cancer: 2018 Diary Pages   71

12 Cancer: 2018 In Brief   72

13 Rising Signs for Cancer   157

14 The Zodiac, Planets and Correspondences   159

INTRODUCTION

Your Personal Horoscopes have been specifically created to allow you to get the most from astrological patterns and the way they have a bearing on not only your zodiac sign, but nuances within it. Using the diary section of the book you can read about the influences and possibilities of each and every day of the year. It will be possible for you to see when you are likely to be cheerful and happy or those times when your nature is in retreat and you will be more circumspect. The diary will help to give you a feel for the specific 'cycles' of astrology and the way they can subtly change your day-to-day life. For example, when you see the sign ☿, this means that the planet Mercury is retrograde at that time. Retrograde means it appears to be running backwards through the zodiac. Such a happening has a significant effect on communication skills, but this is only one small aspect of how the Personal Horoscope can help you.

With Your Personal Horoscope the story doesn't end with the diary pages. It includes simple ways for you to work out the zodiac sign the Moon occupied at the time of your birth, and what this means for your personality. In addition, if you know the time of day you were born, it is possible to discover your Ascendant, yet another important guide to your personal make-up and potential.

Many readers are interested in relationships and in knowing how well they get on with people of other astrological signs. You might also be interested in the way you appear to very different sorts of individuals. If you are such a person, the section on Venus will be of particular interest. Despite the rapidly changing position of this planet, you can work out your Venus sign, and learn what bearing it will have on your life.

Using Your Personal Horoscope you can travel on one of the most fascinating and rewarding journeys that anyone can take – the journey to a better realisation of self.

THE ESSENCE OF CANCER

Exploring the Personality of Cancer the Crab

(22ND JUNE – 22ND JULY)

What's in a sign?

The most obvious fact about you, particularly when viewed by others, is that you are trustworthy. Sometimes this fact gets on your nerves. Many Cancerians long to be bigger, bolder and more ruthless, but it simply isn't the way you were made. You are basically ruled by your emotions and there is very little you can do to get away from the fact. Once you realise this you could be in for a happy life but there are bound to be some frustrations on the way.

Your ruling planet is the Moon, which changes its position in astrological terms far more quickly than any other heavenly body. That's why you can sometimes feel that you have experienced a whole year's emotions in only a month. However the saving grace of this fact is that unlike the other Water signs of Scorpio and Pisces, you are rarely bogged down by emotional restraints for more than a day or two at a time. This gives you a more optimistic attitude and a determination to use your natural talents to the full, even in the face of some adversity. Caring for others is second nature to you and forms a very large part of your life and character.

Your attitude towards romance fluctuates but is generally of the 'story book' sort. Once you commit yourself to another person, either romantically or practically, you are not likely to change your mind very easily. Loyalty is part of what you are about and doesn't change just because things sometimes get a little complicated. Even when you don't really know where you are going, you are inclined to pull those you love along the path with you, and you can usually rely on their assistance. Basically you are very easy to love and there can't be anything much wrong with that fact. At the same time you can be very practical, don't mind doing some of the dirty work and are in your element when those around you are floundering.

The creative potential within your nature is strong. You are a natural homemaker and tend to get a great deal from simply watching others succeed. All the same this isn't the whole story because you are complex and inclined to be too worrisome.

Cancer resources

Your ruling planet is the Moon, Earth's closest neighbour in space. This means that you are as subject to its tides and fluctuations as is our planet. Of course this is a double-edged sword because you can sometimes be an emotional maelstrom inside. To compensate for this fact you have a level of personal sensitivity that would be admired by many. At the same time you have a deep intuition and can usually be relied upon to see through the mist of everyday life and to work out how situations are likely to mature. This is especially true when it comes to assessing those around you.

As a homemaker you are second to none. You can make a few pounds go a very long way and can cope well in circumstances that would greatly trouble those around you. Adversity is not something that bothers you too much at all and it is clear that you can even revel in difficulty. Nothing is too much trouble when you are dealing with people you really love – which includes friends as well as family members.

One of the greatest Cancerian resources is the ability to bring a practical face to even difficult circumstances. Physically speaking you are very resilient, even if you don't always seem to be the strongest person around in an emotional sense. You are given to showing extreme kindness, sometimes even in the face of cruelty from others, though if you are genuinely provoked you can show an anger that would shock most people, even those who think they know you very well indeed.

What really counts the most is your ability to bring others round to your point of view and to get them to do what you think is best. Working from example you won't generally expect others to do anything you are not prepared to try yourself, and your attitude can be an inspiration to others. Through hard work and perseverance you can build a good life for yourself, though your consideration for those around you never diminishes and so even a fortune gained would generally be used on behalf of the world around you. The greatest resource that you possess is your capacity to love and to nurture. This makes you successful and well loved by others.

Beneath the surface

The most difficult aspect of those born under the sign of Cancer the Crab is trying to work out the psychological motivations of this apparently simple but actually deeply complex zodiac position. 'Emotion' is clearly the keyword and is the fountain from which everything, good and bad alike, flows. Whilst some zodiac sign types are inclined to act and then consider the consequences, the Crab is a different beast altogether. The main quality of Cancer is caring. This applies as much to the world at large as it does in consideration of family, though to the Crab it's clear that under almost all circumstances family comes first.

You are a deep thinker and don't always find it easy to explain the way your mind is working. The reason for this is not so difficult to understand. Feelings are not the same as thoughts and it is sometimes quite difficult to express the qualities that rule you internally. What you seem to prefer to do is to put a caring arm around the world and express your inner compassion in this manner. You might also sometimes be a little anxious that if others knew how your innermost mind worked you would become more vulnerable than you already are – which is why the Crab wears a shell in the first place.

At the first sign of emotional pressure from outside you are inclined to retreat into yourself. As a result you don't always confront issues that would be best dealt with immediately. This proclivity runs deep and strong in your nature and can sometimes cause you much more trouble than would be the case if you just made the right statements and asked the correct questions. Physically and mentally you are not inclined to withdraw because you are very much stronger than the world would give you credit for.

Cancerians have a tremendous capacity to love, allied to a potential for positive action when the lives or well-being of others is threatened. In some ways you are the bravest zodiac sign of all because you will march forward into the very gates of hell if you know that you can be of service to those around you. From family to village or town, from town to nation and from nation to a global awareness, yours is the zodiac sign that best epitomises humanity's struggle for a universal understanding.

Making the best of yourself

If you start out from the premise that you are well liked by most people then you are halfway towards any intended destination. Of course you don't always register your popularity and are given to worrying about the impression you give. The picture you paint of yourself is usually very different from the one the world at large sees. If you doubt this, ask some of your best friends to describe your nature and you will be quite surprised. You need to be as open as possible to avoid internalising matters that would be best brought into a more public arena. Your natural tendency to look after everyone else masks a desire to get on in life personally, and the Cancerians who succeed the best are the ones who have somehow managed to bring a sense of balance to their giving and taking.

Try to avoid being too quiet. In social situations you have much to offer, though would rarely do so in a particularly gregarious manner. Nevertheless, and partly because you don't shoot your mouth off all the time, people are willing to listen to what you have to say. Once you realise how strong your influence can be you are already on the road to riches – financial and personal.

Use your imagination to the full because it is one of the most potent weapons in your personal armoury. People won't underestimate you when they know how strong you really are and that means that life can sometimes be less of a struggle. But under most circumstances be your usual warm self, and the love you desire will come your way.

The very practical issues of life are easy for you to deal with, which is why your material success is generally assured. All that is needed to make the picture complete is more confidence in your ability to lead and less inclination to follow.

The impressions you give

There is no doubt at all that you are one of the most loved and the most admired people around. It isn't hard to see why. Your relatives and friends alike feel very protected and loved, which has got to be a good start when it comes to your contacts with the world at large.

The most intriguing thing about being a Cancerian subject is how different you appear to be when viewed by others as against the way you judge your own personality. This is down to external appearances as much as anything. For starters you usually wear a cheery smile, even on those occasions when it is clear you are not smiling inside. You give yourself fully to the needs and wants of those around you and are very sympathetic, even towards strangers. It's true that you may not fully exploit the implications of your pleasant nature – but that's only another typical part of your character.

Those people who know you the best are aware that you have a great capacity to worry about things, and they may also understand that you are rarely as confident as you give the external impression of being. They sense the deeply emotional quality of your nature and can observe the long periods of deep thought. When it comes to the practicalities of life, however, you perhaps should not be surprised that you are sometimes put on rather too much. Even this is understandable because you rarely say no and will usually make yourself available when there is work to be done.

True success for the Cancer subject lies in recognising your strong points and in being willing to gain from them in a personal sense from time to time. You also need to realise that, to others, the impression you give is what you really are. Bridging the gap between outward calm and inner confusion might be the most important lesson.

The way forward

Although you don't always feel quite as sure of yourself as you give the impression of being, you can still exploit your external appearance to your own and other people's advantage. Your strong sense of commitment to family and your ability to get on well in personal relationships are both factors that improve your ability to progress in life.

Achieving a sense of balance is important. For example you can spend long hours locked into your own thoughts, but this isn't good for you in an exclusive sense. Playing out some of your fantasies in the real world can do you good, even though you are aware that this involves taking chances, something you don't always care to do. At the same time you should not be afraid to make gains as a result of the way you are loved by others. This doesn't come for free and you work long and hard to establish the affection that comes your way.

In practical matters you are capable and well able to get on in life. Money comes your way, not usually as a result of particularly good luck, but because you are a tireless and steady worker. You can accept responsibility, even though the implied management side of things worries you somewhat. To have a career is important because it broadens your outlook and keeps you functioning in the wider world, which is where your personal successes take place. The more you achieve, the greater is the level of confidence that you feel – which in turn leads to even greater progress.

Cancerians should never cut themselves off from the mainstream of life. It's true you have many acquaintances but very few really close friends, but that doesn't matter. Practically everyone you know is pleased to name you as a trusted ally, which has to be the best compliment of all to your apparently serene and settled nature.

In love you are ardent and sincere. It may take you a while to get round to expressing the way you feel, partly because you are a little afraid of failure in this most important area of your life. All the same you love with a passion and are supportive to your partner. Family will always be the most important sphere of life because your zodiac sign rules the astrological fourth house, which is essentially dedicated to home and family matters. If you are contented in this arena it tends to show in other areas of your life too. Your affable nature is your best friend and only tends to disappear if you allow yourself to become too stressed.

CANCER ON THE CUSP

Astrological profiles are altered for those people born at either the beginning or the end of a zodiac sign, or, more properly, on the cusps of a sign. In the case of Cancer this would be on the 22nd of June and for two or three days after, and similarly at the end of the sign, probably from the 20th to the 22nd of July.

The Gemini Cusp – June 22nd to June 24th

You are certainly fun to be around and the sign of Gemini has a great deal to do with your basic motivations. As a result, you tend to be slightly more chatty than the average Cancerian and usually prove to be the life and soul of any party that is going on in your vicinity. Not everyone understands the basic sensitivity that lies below the surface of this rather brash exterior, however, and you can sometimes be a little hurt if people take you absolutely at face value.

There probably isn't the total consistency of emotional responses that one generally expects to find in the Crab when taken alone, and there are times when you might be accused of being rather fickle. All the same, you have a big heart and show genuine concern for anyone in trouble, especially the underdog. Your Gemini attributes give you the opportunity to speak your mind, so when it comes to aiding the world you can be a tireless reformer and show a great ability to think before you speak, which is not typical of Gemini on its own, although there are occasions when the two sides of your nature tend to be at odds with each other.

At work you are very capable and can be relied upon to make instant decisions whenever necessary. Your executive capabilities are pronounced and you are more than capable of thinking on your feet, even if you prefer to mull things over if possible. You are the sort of person that others tend to rely on for advice and will not usually let your colleagues or friends down.

In matters of love, you are less steadfast and loyal than the Crab, yet you care very deeply for your loved ones. People like to have you around and actively seek your advice which, in the main, is considered and sound, though always delivered with humour. You love to travel and would never wish to be limited in either your horizons or your lifestyle. All in all, you are a fun person, good to know, and basically sensible.

The Leo Cusp – July 20th to July 22nd

Here we find a Cancerian who tends to know what he or she wants from life. Part of the natural tendency of the Crab is to be fairly shy and retiring, though progressively less so as the Sun moves on towards the sign of Leo. You are probably aware that you don't exactly match the Cancer stereotype and are likely to be more outspoken, determined and even argumentative at times. You have lofty ideals, which find a ready home for the sensitive qualities that you draw from Cancer. Many social reformers tend to have their Suns very close to the Leo cusp of Cancer and people born on this cusp like to work hard for the world, especially for the less well-off members of society.

In matters of love, you are deep, but ardent and sincere, finding better ways of expressing your emotions verbally than those generally associated with the Crab. You are capable at work, easily able to take on responsibilities that involve controlling other people, and you are outwardly braver than often seems to be the case with Cancer alone. Not everyone finds you particularly easy to understand, probably because there are some definite paradoxes about your nature.

A few problems come along in the area of ideals, which are more important to you than they would be to some of the people with whom you associate. You need to be sure of yourself, a fact that leads to fairly long thinking periods, but once you have formed a particular belief you will move heaven and earth to demonstrate how sensible it is. Don't be too alarmed if not everyone agrees with you.

You are not the typical conformist that might more usually be the case with Cancerians, and feel the need to exercise your civic rights to the full. Tireless when dealing with something you think is especially important, you are a good and loyal friend, a staunch and steadfast lover and you care deeply about your family. However, you are not as confrontational as a person born completely under Leo, and therefore can usually be relied upon to seek a compromise.

CANCER AND ITS ASCENDANTS

The nature of every individual on the planet is composed of the rich variety of zodiac signs and planetary positions that were present at the time of their birth. Your Sun sign, which in your case is Cancer, is one of the many factors when it comes to assessing the unique person you are. Probably the most important consideration, other than your Sun sign, is to establish the zodiac sign that was rising over the eastern horizon at the time that you were born. This is your Ascending or Rising sign. Most popular astrology fails to take account of the Ascendant, and yet its importance remains with you from the very moment of your birth, through every day of your life. The Ascendant is evident in the way you approach the world, and so, when meeting a person for the first time, it is this astrological influence that you are most likely to notice first. Our Ascending sign essentially represents what we appear to be, while the Sun sign is what we feel inside ourselves.

The Ascendant also has the potential for modifying our overall nature. For example, if you were born at a time of day when Cancer was passing over the eastern horizon (this would be around the time of dawn) then you would be classed as a double Cancerian. As such, you would typify this zodiac sign, both internally and in your dealings with others. However, if your Ascendant sign turned out to be a Fire sign, such as Aries, there would be a profound alteration of nature, away from the expected qualities of Cancer.

One of the reasons why popular astrology often ignores the Ascendant is that it has always been rather difficult to establish. We have found a way to make this possible by devising an easy-to-use table, which you will find on page 157 of this book. Using this, you can establish your Ascendant sign at a glance. You will need to know your rough time of birth, then it is simply a case of following the instructions.

For those readers who have no idea of their time of birth it might be worth allowing a good friend, or perhaps your partner, to read through the section that follows this introduction. Someone who deals with you on a regular basis may easily discover your Ascending sign, even though you could have some difficulty establishing it for yourself. A good understanding of this component of your nature is essential if you want to be aware of that 'other person' who is responsible for the way you make contact with the world at large. Your Sun sign, Ascendant sign, and the other pointers in this book will, together, allow you a far better understanding of what makes you tick as an individual. Peeling back the different layers of your astrological make-up can be an enlightening experience, and the Ascendant may represent one of the most important layers of all.

Cancer with Cancer Ascendant

You are one of the most warm and loving individuals that it is possible to know, and you carry a quiet dignity that few would fail to recognise. Getting on with things in your own steady way, you are, nevertheless, capable of great things, simply because you keep going. Even in the face of adversity your steady but relentless pace can be observed, and much of what you do is undertaken on behalf of those you love the most. On the other side of the coin you represent something of a mystery and it is also true that emotionally speaking you tend to be very highly charged. It doesn't take much to bring you to tears and you are inclined to have a special affection for the underdog, which on occasions can get you into a little trouble. Although it is your natural way to keep a low profile, you will speak out loudly if you think that anyone you care for is under attack, and yet you don't show the same tendency on your own behalf.

Rarely if ever out of control, you are the levelling influence everyone feels they need in their life, which is one of the reasons why you are so loved. Your quiet ways are accepted by the world, which is why some people will be astonished when you suddenly announce that you are about to travel overland to Asia. What a great puzzle you can be, but that is half the attraction.

Cancer with Leo Ascendant

This can be a very fortunate combination, for when seen at its best it brings all the concern and the natural caring qualities of Cancer, allied to the more dynamic and very brave face of Leo. Somehow there is a great deal of visible energy here, but it manifests itself in a way that always shows a concern for the world at large. No matter what charitable works are going on in your district it is likely that you will be involved in one way or another, and you relish the cut and thrust of life much more than the retiring side of Cancer would seem to do. You are quite capable of walking alone and don't really need the company of others for large chunks of the average day. However, when you are in social situations you fare very well and can usually be observed with a smile on your face.

Conversationally speaking you have sound, considered opinions and often represent the voice of steady wisdom when faced with a situation that means arbitration. In fact you will often be put in this situation, and there is more than one politician and union representative who shares this undeniably powerful zodiac combination. Like all those associated with the sign of Cancer you love to travel and can make a meal out of your journeys with brave, intrepid Leo lending a hand in both the planning and the doing.

Cancer with Virgo Ascendant

What can this union of zodiac signs bring to the party that isn't there in either Cancer or Virgo alone? Well, quite a bit actually. Virgo can be very fussy on occasions and too careful for its own good. The presence of steady, serene Cancer alters the perspectives and allows a smoother, more flowing individual to greet the world. You are chatty and easy to know, and exhibit a combination of the practical skills of Virgo, together with the deep and penetrating insights that are typical of Cancer. This can make you appear to be very powerful and your insights are second to none. You are a born organiser and love to be where things are happening, even if you are only there to help make the sandwiches or to pour the tea. Invariably your role will be much greater but you don't seek personal acclaim and are a good team player on most occasions.

There is a quiet side to your nature and those who live with you will eventually get used to your need for solitude. This seems strange because Virgo is generally such a chatterbox and, taken on its own, is rarely quiet for long. In matters of love you show great affection and a sense of responsibility that makes you an ideal parent. It is sometimes the case, however, that you care rather more than you should be willing to show.

Cancer with Libra Ascendant

What an absolutely pleasant and approachable sort of person you are, and how much you have to offer. Like most people associated with the sign of Cancer, you give yourself freely to the world and will always be on hand if anyone is in trouble or needs the special touch you can bring to almost any problem. Behaving in this way is the biggest part of what you are and so people come to rely on you very heavily. Like Libra you can see both sides of any coin and you exhibit the Libran tendency to jump about from one foot to the other when it is necessary to make decisions relating to your own life. This is not usually the case when you are dealing with others, however, because the cooler and more detached qualities of Cancer will show through in these circumstances.

It would be fair to say that you do not deal with routines as well as Cancer alone might do and you need a degree of variety in your life. In your case this possibly comes in the form of travel, which can be distant and of long duration. It isn't unusual for people who have this zodiac combination to end up living abroad, though even this does little to prevent you from getting itchy feet from time to time. In relationships you show an original quality that keeps the relationship young, fresh and working well.

Cancer with Scorpio Ascendant

There are few more endearing zodiac combinations than this. Both signs are Watery in nature and show a desire to work on behalf of humanity as a whole. The world sees you as being genuinely caring, full of sympathy for anyone in trouble and always ready to lend a hand when it is needed. You are a loyal friend, a great supporter of the oppressed and a lover of home and family. In a work sense you are capable and command respect from your colleagues, even though this comes about courtesy of your quiet competence, and not as a result of anything that you might happen to say or do.

But we should not get too carried away with external factors, or the way that others see you. Inside you are a boiling pool of emotion. You feel more strongly, love more deeply and hurt more fully than any other combination of the Water signs. Even those who think that they know you really well would get a shock if they could take a stroll around the deeper recesses of your mind. Although these facts are true, they may be rather beside the point because the truth of your passion, commitment and deep convictions may only surface fully half a dozen times in your life. The fact is that you are a very private person at heart and you don't know how to be any other way.

Cancer with Sagittarius Ascendant

You have far more drive, enthusiasm and get-up-and-go than would seem to be the case for Cancer when taken alone, but all of this is tempered with a certain quiet compassion that probably makes you the best sort of Sagittarian too. It's true that you don't like to be on your own or to retire into your shell quite as much as the Crab usually does, though there are, even in your case, occasions when this is going to be necessary. Absolute concentration can sometimes be a problem to you, though this is hardly likely to be the case when you are dealing with matters relating to your home or family, both of which reign supreme in your thinking. Always loving and kind, you are a social animal and enjoy being out there in the real world, expressing the deeper opinions of Cancer much more readily than would often be the case with other combinations relating to the sign of the Crab.

Personality is not lacking, and you tend to be very popular, not least because you are the fountain of good and practical advice. You want to get things done, and retain a practical approach to most situations which is the envy of many of the people you meet. As a parent you are second to none, combining common sense, dignity and a sensible approach. To balance this you stay young enough to understand children.

Cancer with Capricorn Ascendant

The single most important factor here is the practical ability to get things done and to see any task, professional or personal, through to the end. Since half this combination is Cancer, that also means expounding much of your energy on behalf of others. There isn't a charity in the world that would fail to recognise what a potent combination this is when it comes to the very concrete side of offering help and assistance. Many of your ideas hold water and you don't set off on abortive journeys of any kind, simply because you tend to get the ground rules fixed in your mind first.

On a more personal level you can be rather hard to get to know, because both these signs have a deep quality and a tendency to keep things in the dark. The mystery may only serve to encourage people to try and get to know you better. As a result you could attract a host of admirers, many of whom would wish to form romantic attachments. This may prove to be irrelevant, however, because once you give your heart, you tend to be loyal and would only change your mind if you were pushed into doing so. Prolonged periods of inactivity don't do you any good and it is sensible for you to keep on the move, even though your progress in life is measured and very steady.

CANCER AND ITS ASCENDANTS

Cancer with Aquarius Ascendant

The truly original spark, for which the sign of Aquarius is famed, can only enhance the caring qualities of Cancer, and is also inclined to bring the Crab out of its shell to a much greater extent than would be the case with certain other zodiac combinations. Aquarius is a party animal and never arrives without something interesting to say, which is doubly so when the reservoir of emotion and consideration that is Cancer is feeding the tap. Your nature can be rather confusing, even for you to deal with, but you are inspirational, bright, charming and definitely fun to be around.

The Cancer element in your nature means that you care about your home and the people to whom you are related. You are also a good and loyal friend, who would keep attachments for much longer than could be expected for Aquarius alone. You love to travel and can be expected to make many journeys to far-off places during your life. Some attention will have to be paid to your health because you are capable of burning up masses of nervous energy, often without getting the periods of rest and contemplation that are essential to the deeper qualities of the sign of Cancer. Nevertheless you have determination, resilience and a refreshing attitude that lifts the spirits of the people in your vicinity.

25

Cancer with Pisces Ascendant

A deep, double Water-sign combination, this one, and it might serve to make you a very misunderstood, though undoubtedly popular, individual. You are keen to make a good impression, probably too keen under certain circumstances, and you do everything you can to help others, even if you don't know them very well. It's true that you are deeply sensitive and quite easily brought to tears by the suffering of this most imperfect world that we inhabit. Fatigue can be a problem, though this is nullified to some extent by the fact that you can withdraw completely into the deep recesses of your own mind when it becomes necessary to do so.

You may not be the most gregarious person in the world, simply because it isn't easy for you to put your most important considerations into words. This is easier when you are in the company of people you know and trust, though even trust is a commodity that is difficult for you to find, particularly since you may have been hurt by being too willing to share your thoughts early in life. With age comes wisdom and maturity and the older you are, the better you will learn to handle this potent and demanding combination. You will never go short of either friends or would-be lovers, and may be one of the most magnetic types of both Cancer and Pisces.

Cancer with Aries Ascendant

The main problem that you experience in life shows itself as a direct result of the meshing of these two very different zodiac signs. At heart Aries needs to dominate, whereas Cancer shows a desire to nurture. All too often the result can be a protective arm that is so strong that nobody could possibly get out from under it. Lighten your own load, and that of those you care for, by being willing to sit back and watch others please themselves a little. You might think that you know best, and your heart is clearly in the right place, but try and realise what life can be like when someone is always on hand to tell you that they know better than you do.

But in a way this is a little severe, because you are fairly intuitive and your instincts will rarely lead you astray. Nobody could ask for a better partner or parent than you would be, though they might request a slightly less attentive one. In matters of work you are conscientious, and are probably best suited to a job that means sorting out the kind of mess that humanity is so good at creating. You probably spend your spare time untangling balls of wool, though you are quite sporting too and could even make the Olympics. Once there you would not win however, because you would be too concerned about all the other competitors!

Cancer with Taurus Ascendant

Your main aim in life seems to be to look after everyone and everything that you come across. From your deepest and most enduring human love, right down to the birds in the park, you really do care and you show that natural affection in many different ways. Your nature is sensitive and you are easily moved to tears, though this does not prevent you from pitching in and doing practical things to assist at just about any level. There is a danger that you could stifle those same people whom you set out to assist, and people with this zodiac combination are often unwilling, or unable, to allow their children to grow and leave the nest. More time spent considering what suits you would be no bad thing, but the problem is that you find it almost impossible to imagine any situation that doesn't involve your most basic need, which is to nurture.

You appear not to possess a selfish streak, though it sometimes turns out that in being certain that you understand the needs of the world, you are nevertheless treading on their toes. This eventual realisation can be very painful, but it isn't a stick with which you should beat yourself because at heart you are one of the kindest people imaginable. Your sense of fair play means that you are a quiet social reformer at heart.

Cancer with Gemini Ascendant

Many astrologers would say that this is a happy combination because some of the more flighty qualities of Gemini are somewhat modified by the steady influence of Cancer the Crab. To all intents and purposes you show the friendly and gregarious qualities of Gemini, but there is a thoughtful and even sometimes a serious quality that would not be present in Gemini when taken alone. Looking after people is high on your list of priorities and you do this most of the time. This is made possible because you have greater staying power than Gemini is usually said to possess and you can easily see fairly complicated situations through to their conclusion without becoming bored on the way.

The chances are that you will have many friends and that these people show great concern for your well-being, because you choose them carefully and show them a great deal of consideration. However, you will still be on the receiving end of gossip on occasions, and need to treat such situations with a healthy pinch of salt. Like all part-Geminis your nervous system is not as strong as you would wish to believe and family pressures in particular can put great strain on you. Activities of all kinds take your fancy and many people with this combination are attracted to sailing or wind surfing.

THE MOON AND THE PART IT PLAYS IN YOUR LIFE

In astrology the Moon is probably the single most important heavenly body after the Sun. Its unique position, as partner to the Earth on its journey around the solar system, means that the Moon appears to pass through the signs of the zodiac extremely quickly. The zodiac position of the Moon at the time of your birth plays a great part in personal character and is especially significant in the build-up of your emotional nature.

Your Own Moon Sign

Discovering the position of the Moon at the time of your birth has always been notoriously difficult because tracking the complex zodiac positions of the Moon is not easy. This process has been reduced to three simple stages with our Lunar Tables. A breakdown of the Moon's zodiac positions can be found from page 35 onwards, so that once you know what your Moon Sign is, you can see what part this plays in the overall build-up of your personal character.

If you follow the instructions on the next page you will soon be able to work out exactly what zodiac sign the Moon occupied on the day that you were born and you can then go on to compare the reading for this position with those of your Sun sign and your Ascendant. It is partly the comparison between these three important positions that goes towards making you the unique individual you are.

HOW TO DISCOVER YOUR MOON SIGN

This is a three-stage process. You may need a pen and a piece of paper but if you follow the instructions below the process should only take a minute or so.

STAGE 1 First of all you need to know the Moon Age at the time of your birth. If you look at Moon Table 1, on page 33, you will find all the years between 1920 and 2018 down the left side. Find the year of your birth and then trace across to the right to the month of your birth. Where the two intersect you will find a number. This is the date of the New Moon in the month that you were born. You now need to count forward the number of days between the New Moon and your own birthday. For example, if the New Moon in the month of your birth was shown as being the 6th and you were born on the 20th, your Moon Age Day would be 14. If the New Moon in the month of your birth came after your birthday, you need to count forward from the New Moon in the previous month. Whatever the result, jot this number down so that you do not forget it.

STAGE 2 Take a look at Moon Table 2 on page 34. Down the left hand column look for the date of your birth. Now trace across to the month of your birth. Where the two meet you will find a letter. Copy this letter down alongside your Moon Age Day.

STAGE 3 Moon Table 3 on page 34 will supply you with the zodiac sign the Moon occupied on the day of your birth. Look for your Moon Age Day down the left hand column and then for the letter you found in Stage 2. Where the two converge you will find a zodiac sign and this is the sign occupied by the Moon on the day that you were born.

Your Zodiac Moon Sign Explained

You will find a profile of all zodiac Moon Signs on pages 35 to 38, showing in yet another way how astrology helps to make you into the individual that you are. In each daily entry of the Astral Diary you can find the zodiac position of the Moon for every day of the year. This also allows you to discover your lunar birthdays. Since the Moon passes through all the signs of the zodiac in about a month, you can expect something like twelve lunar birthdays each year. At these times you are likely to be emotionally steady and able to make the sort of decisions that have real, lasting value.

MOON TABLE 1

YEAR	MAY	JUN	JUL	YEAR	MAY	JUN	JUL	YEAR	MAY	JUN	JUL
1920	18	16	15	1953	13	11	11	1986	8	7	7
1921	7	6	5	1954	2	1/30	29	1987	27	26	25
1922	26	25	24	1955	21	20	19	1988	15	14	13
1923	15	14	14	1956	10	8	8	1989	5	3	3
1924	3	2	2/31	1957	29	27	27	1990	24	22	22
1925	22	21	20	1958	18	17	16	1991	13	11	11
1926	11	10	9	1959	7	6	6	1992	2	1/30	29
1927	2/31	29	28	1960	26	24	24	1993	21	19	19
1928	19	18	17	1961	14	13	12	1994	10	8	8
1929	9	7	6	1962	4	2	1/31	1995	29	27	27
1930	28	26	25	1963	23	21	20	1996	18	17	15
1931	17	16	15	1964	11	10	9	1997	6	5	4
1932	5	4	3	1965	1/30	29	28	1998	25	24	23
1933	24	23	22	1966	19	18	17	1999	15	13	13
1934	13	12	11	1967	8	7	7	2000	4	2	1/31
1935	2	1/30	30	1968	27	26	25	2001	23	21	20
1936	20	19	18	1969	15	14	13	2002	12	10	9
1937	10	8	8	1970	6	4	4	2003	1/30	29	28
1938	29	27	27	1971	24	22	22	2004	18	16	16
1939	19	17	16	1972	13	11	11	2005	8	6	6
1940	7	6	5	1973	2	1/30	29	2006	27	26	25
1941	26	24	24	1974	21	20	19	2007	17	17	15
1942	15	13	13	1975	11	9	9	2008	5	4	3
1943	4	2	2	1976	29	27	27	2009	25	23	22
1944	22	20	20	1977	18	16	16	2010	14	12	12
1945	11	10	9	1978	7	5	5	2011	3	2	2
1946	1/30	29	28	1979	26	24	24	2012	20	19	19
1947	19	18	17	1980	14	13	12	2013	10	8	7
1948	9	7	6	1981	4	2	1/31	2014	29	27	25
1949	27	26	25	1982	21	21	20	2015	18	17	16
1950	17	15	15	1983	12	11	10	2016	6	4	4
1951	6	4	4	1984	1/30	29	28	2017	25	24	23
1952	23	22	22	1985	19	18	17	2018	15	13	13

TABLE 2   MOON TABLE 3

DAY	JUN	JUL	M/D	O	P	Q	R	S	T	U
1	O	R	0	GE	GE	CA	CA	CA	LE	LE
2	P	R	1	GE	CA	CA	CA	LE	LE	LE
3	P	S	2	CA	CA	CA	LE	LE	LE	VI
4	P	S	3	CA	CA	LE	LE	LE	VI	VI
5	P	S	4	LE	LE	LE	LE	VI	VI	LI
6	P	S	5	LE	LE	VI	VI	VI	LI	LI
7	P	S	6	VI	VI	VI	VI	LI	LI	LI
8	P	S	7	VI	VI	LI	LI	LI	LI	SC
9	P	S	8	VI	VI	LI	LI	LI	SC	SC
10	P	S	9	LI	LI	SC	SC	SC	SC	SA
11	P	S	10	LI	LI	SC	SC	SC	SA	SA
12	Q	S	11	SC	SC	SC	SA	SA	SA	CP
13	Q	T	12	SC	SC	SA	SA	SA	SA	CP
14	Q	T	13	SC	SA	SA	SA	SA	CP	CP
15	Q	T	14	SA	SA	SA	CP	CP	CP	AQ
16	Q	T	15	SA	SA	CP	CP	CP	AQ	AQ
17	Q	T	16	CP	CP	CP	AQ	AQ	AQ	AQ
18	Q	T	17	CP	CP	CP	AQ	AQ	AQ	PI
19	Q	T	18	CP	CP	AQ	AQ	AQ	PI	PI
20	Q	T	19	AQ	AQ	AQ	PI	PI	PI	PI
21	Q	T	20	AQ	AQ	PI	PI	PI	AR	AR
22	R	T	21	AQ	PI	PI	PI	AR	AR	AR
23	R	T	22	PI	PI	PI	AR	AR	AR	TA
24	R	U	23	PI	PI	AR	AR	AR	TA	TA
25	R	U	24	PI	AR	AR	AR	TA	TA	TA
26	R	U	25	AR	AR	TA	TA	TA	GE	GE
27	R	U	26	AR	TA	TA	TA	GE	GE	GE
28	R	U	27	TA	TA	TA	GE	GE	GE	CA
29	R	U	28	TA	TA	GE	GE	GE	CA	CA
30	R	U	29	TA	GE	GE	GE	CA	CA	CA
31	–	U								

AR = Aries, TA = Taurus, GE = Gemini, CA = Cancer, LE = Leo, VI = Virgo,
LI = Libra, SC = Scorpio, SA = Sagittarius, CP = Capricorn, AQ = Aquarius, PI = Pisces

MOON SIGNS

Moon in Aries

You have a strong imagination, courage, determination and a desire to do things in your own way and forge your own path through life.

Originality is a key attribute; you are seldom stuck for ideas although your mind is changeable and you could take the time to focus on individual tasks. Often quick-tempered, you take orders from few people and live life at a fast pace. Avoid health problems by taking regular time out for rest and relaxation.

Emotionally, it is important that you talk to those you are closest to and work out your true feelings. Once you discover that people are there to help, there is less necessity for you to do everything yourself.

Moon in Taurus

The Moon in Taurus gives you a courteous and friendly manner, which means you are likely to have many friends.

The good things in life mean a lot to you, as Taurus is an Earth sign that delights in experiences which please the senses. Hence you are probably a lover of good food and drink, which may in turn mean you need to keep an eye on the bathroom scales, especially as looking good is also important to you.

Emotionally you are fairly stable and you stick by your own standards. Taureans do not respond well to change. Intuition also plays an important part in your life.

Moon in Gemini

You have a warm-hearted character, sympathetic and eager to help others. At times reserved, you can also be articulate and chatty: this is part of the paradox of Gemini, which always brings duplicity to the nature. You are interested in current affairs, have a good intellect, and are good company and likely to have many friends. Most of your friends have a high opinion of you and would be ready to defend you should the need arise. However, this is usually unnecessary, as you are quite capable of defending yourself in any verbal confrontation.

Travel is important to your inquisitive mind and you find intellectual stimulus in mixing with people from different cultures. You also gain much from reading, writing and the arts but you do need plenty of rest and relaxation in order to avoid fatigue.

Moon in Cancer

The Moon in Cancer at the time of birth is a fortunate position as Cancer is the Moon's natural home. This means that the qualities of compassion and understanding given by the Moon are especially enhanced in your nature, and you are friendly and sociable and cope well with emotional pressures. You cherish home and family life, and happily do the domestic tasks. Your surroundings are important to you and you hate squalor and filth. You are likely to have a love of music and poetry.

Your basic character, although at times changeable like the Moon itself, depends on symmetry. You aim to make your surroundings comfortable and harmonious, for yourself and those close to you.

Moon in Leo

The best qualities of the Moon and Leo come together to make you warm-hearted, fair, ambitious and self-confident. With good organisational abilities, you invariably rise to a position of responsibility in your chosen career. This is fortunate as you don't enjoy being an 'also-ran' and would rather be an important part of a small organisation than a menial in a large one.

You should be lucky in love, and happy, provided you put in the effort to make a comfortable home for yourself and those close to you. It is likely that you will have a love of pleasure, sport, music and literature. Life brings you many rewards, most of them as a direct result of your own efforts, although you may be luckier than average and ready to make the best of any situation.

Moon in Virgo

You are endowed with good mental abilities and a keen receptive memory, but you are never ostentatious or pretentious. Naturally quite reserved, you still have many friends, especially of the opposite sex. Marital relationships must be discussed carefully and worked at so that they remain harmonious, as personal attachments can be a problem if you do not give them your full attention.

Talented and persevering, you possess artistic qualities and are a good homemaker. Earning your honours through genuine merit, you work long and hard towards your objectives but show little pride in your achievements. Many short journeys will be undertaken in your life.

Moon in Libra

With the Moon in Libra you are naturally popular and make friends easily. People like you, probably more than you realise, you bring fun to a party and are a natural diplomat. For all its good points, Libra is not the most stable of astrological signs and, as a result, your emotions can be a little unstable too. Therefore, although the Moon in Libra is said to be good for love and marriage, your Sun sign and Rising sign will have an important effect on your emotional and loving qualities.

You must remember to relate to others in your decision-making. Co-operation is crucial because Libra represents the 'balance' of life that can only be achieved through harmonious relationships. Conformity is not easy for you because Libra, an Air sign, likes its independence.

Moon in Scorpio

Some people might call you pushy. In fact, all you really want to do is to live life to the full and protect yourself and your family from the pressures of life. Take care to avoid giving the impression of being sarcastic or impulsive and use your energies wisely and constructively.

You have great courage and you invariably achieve your goals by force of personality and sheer effort. You are fond of mystery and are good at predicting the outcome of situations and events. Travel experiences can be beneficial to you.

You may experience problems if you do not take time to examine your motives in a relationship, and also if you allow jealousy, always a feature of Scorpio, to cloud your judgement.

Moon in Sagittarius

The Moon in Sagittarius helps to make you a generous individual with humanitarian qualities and a kind heart. Restlessness may be intrinsic as your mind is seldom still. Perhaps because of this, you have a need for change that could lead you to several major moves during your adult life. You are not afraid to stand your ground when you know your judgement is right, you speak directly and have good intuition.

At work you are quick, efficient and versatile and so you make an ideal employee. You need work to be intellectually demanding and do not enjoy tedious routines.

In relationships, you anger quickly if faced with stupidity or deception, though you are just as quick to forgive and forget. Emotionally, there are times when your heart rules your head.

Moon in Capricorn

The Moon in Capricorn makes you popular and likely to come into the public eye in some way. The watery Moon is not entirely comfortable in the Earth sign of Capricorn and this may lead to some difficulties in the early years of life. An initial lack of creative ability and indecision must be overcome before the true qualities of patience and perseverance inherent in Capricorn can show through.

You have good administrative ability and are a capable worker, and if you are careful you can accumulate wealth. But you must be cautious and take professional advice in partnerships, as you are open to deception. You may be interested in social or welfare work, which suit your organisational skills and sympathy for others.

Moon in Aquarius

The Moon in Aquarius makes you an active and agreeable person with a friendly, easy-going nature. Sympathetic to the needs of others, you flourish in a laid-back atmosphere. You are broad-minded, fair and open to suggestion, although sometimes you have an unconventional quality which others can find hard to understand.

You are interested in the strange and curious, and in old articles and places. You enjoy trips to these places and gain much from them. Political, scientific and educational work interests you and you might choose a career in science or technology.

Money-wise, you make gains through innovation and concentration and Lunar Aquarians often tackle more than one job at a time. In love you are kind and honest.

Moon in Pisces

You have a kind, sympathetic nature, somewhat retiring at times, but you always take account of others' feelings and help when you can.

Personal relationships may be problematic, but as life goes on you can learn from your experiences and develop a better understanding of yourself and the world around you.

You have a fondness for travel, appreciate beauty and harmony and hate disorder and strife. You may be fond of literature and would make a good writer or speaker yourself. You have a creative imagination and may come across as an incurable romantic. You have strong intuition, maybe bordering on a mediumistic quality, which sets you apart from the mass. You may not be rich in cash terms, but your personal gifts are worth more than gold.

CANCER IN LOVE

Discover how compatible in love you are with people from the same and other signs of the zodiac. Five stars equals a match made in heaven!

Cancer meets Cancer

This match will work because the couple share a mutual understanding. Cancerians are very kind people who also respond well to kindness from others, so a double Cancer match can almost turn into a mutual appreciation society! But this will not lead to selfish hedonism, as the Crab takes in order to give more. There is an impressive physical, emotional and spiritual meeting of minds, which will lead to a successful and inspiring pairing in its own low-key and deeply sensitive way. Star rating: *****

Cancer meets Leo

This relationship will usually be directed by Leo more towards its own needs than Cancer's. However, the Crab will willingly play second fiddle to more progressive and bossy types as it is deeply emotional and naturally supportive. Leo is bright, caring, magnanimous and protective and so, as long as it isn't over-assertive, this could be a good match. On the surface, Cancer appears the more conventional of the two, but Leo will discover, to its delight, that it can be unusual and quirky. Star rating: ****

Cancer meets Virgo

This match has little chance of success, for fairly simple reasons: Cancer's generous affection will be submerged by the Virgoan depths, not because Virgo is uncaring but because it expresses itself so differently. As both signs are naturally quiet, things might become a bit boring. They would be mutually supportive, possibly financially successful and have a very tidy house, but they won't share much sparkle, enthusiasm, risk-taking or passion. If this pair were stranded on a desert island, they might live at different ends of it. Star rating: **

Cancer meets Libra

Almost anyone can get on with Libra, which is one of the most adaptable signs of them all. But being adaptable does not always lead to fulfilment, and a successful match here will require a quiet Libran and a slightly more progressive Cancerian than the norm. Both signs are pleasant, polite and like domestic order, but Libra may find Cancer too emotional and perhaps lacking in vibrancy, while Libra, on the other hand, may be a little too flighty for steady Cancer. Star rating: ***

Cancer meets Scorpio

This match is potentially a great success, a fact which is often a mystery to astrologers. Some feel it is due to the compatibility of the Water element, but it could also come from a mixture of similarity and difference in the personalities. Scorpio is partly ruled by Mars, which gives it a deep, passionate, dominant and powerful side. Cancerians generally like and respect this amalgam, and recognise something there that they would like to adopt themselves. On the other side of the coin, Scorpio needs love and emotional security which Cancer offers generously. Star rating: *****

Cancer meets Sagittarius

Although probably not an immediate success, there is hope for this couple. It's hard to see how this pair could get together, because they have few mutual interests. Sagittarius is always on the go, loves a hectic social life and dances the night away. Cancer prefers the cinema or a concert. But, having met, Cancer will appreciate the Archer's happy and cheerful nature, while Sagittarius finds Cancer alluring and intriguing and, as the saying goes, opposites attract. A long-term relationship would focus on commitment to family, with Cancer leading this area. Star rating: ***

Cancer meets Capricorn

Just about the only thing this pair have in common is the fact that both signs begin with 'Ca'! Some signs of the zodiac are instigators and some are reactors, and both the Crab and the Goat are reactors. Consequently, they both need incentives from their partners but won't find it in each other and, with neither side taking the initiative, there's a spark missing. Cancer and Capricorn do think alike in some ways and so, if they can find their spark or common purpose, they can be as happy as anyone. It's just rather unlikely. Star rating: **

Cancer meets Aquarius

Cancer is often attracted to Aquarius and, as Aquarius is automatically on the side of anyone who fancies it, so there is the potential for something good here. Cancer loves Aquarius' devil-may-care approach to life, but also recognises and seeks to strengthen the basic lack of self-confidence that all Air signs try so hard to keep secret. Both signs are natural travellers and are quite adventurous. Their family life would be unusual, even peculiar, but friends would recognise a caring, sharing household with many different interests shared by people genuinely in love. Star rating: ***

Cancer meets Pisces

This is likely to be a very successful match. Cancer and Pisces are both Water signs, and are both deep, sensitive and very caring. Pisces loves deeply, and Cancer wants to be loved. There will be few fireworks here, and a very quiet house. But that doesn't mean that either love or action is lacking – the latter of which is just behind closed doors. Family and children are important to both signs and both are prepared to work hard, but Pisces is the more restless of the two and needs the support and security that Cancer offers. Star rating: *****

Cancer meets Aries

A potentially one-sided pairing, it often appears that the Cancerian is brow-beaten by the far more dominant Arian. So much depends on the patience of the Cancerian individual, because if good psychology is present – who knows? But beware, Aries, you may find your partner too passive, and constantly having to take the lead can be wearing – even for you. A prolonged trial period would be advantageous, as the match could easily go either way. When it does work, though, this relationship is usually contented. Star rating: ***

Cancer meets Taurus

This pair will have the tidiest house in the street – every stick of furniture in place, and no errant blade of grass daring to spoil the lawn. But things inside the relationship might not be quite so ship-shape as both signs need, but don't offer, encouragement. There's plenty of affection, but few incentives for mutual progress. This might not prevent material success, but an enduring relationship isn't based on money alone. Passion is essential, and both parties need to realise and aim for that. Star rating: **

Cancer meets Gemini

This is often a very good match. Cancer is a very caring sign and quite adaptable. Geminis are untidy, have butterfly minds and are usually full of a thousand different schemes which Cancerians take in their stride and even relish. They can often be the 'wind beneath the wings' of their Gemini partners. In return, Gemini can eradicate some of the Cancerian emotional insecurity and will be more likely to be faithful in thought, word and deed to Cancer than to almost any other sign. Star rating: ****

VENUS:
THE PLANET OF LOVE

If you look up at the sky around sunset or sunrise you will often see Venus in close attendance to the Sun. It is arguably one of the most beautiful sights of all and there is little wonder that historically it became associated with the goddess of love. But although Venus does play an important part in the way you view love and in the way others see you romantically, this is only one of the spheres of influence that it enjoys in your overall character.

Venus has a part to play in the more cultured side of your life and has much to do with your appreciation of art, literature, music and general creativity. Even the way you look is responsive to the part of the zodiac that Venus occupied at the start of your life, though this fact is also down to your Sun sign and Ascending sign. If, at the time you were born, Venus occupied one of the more gregarious zodiac signs, you will be more likely to wear your heart on your sleeve, as well as to be more attracted to entertainment, social gatherings and good company. If on the other hand Venus occupied a quiet zodiac sign at the time of your birth, you would tend to be more retiring and less willing to shine in public situations.

It's good to know what part the planet Venus plays in your life for it can have a great bearing on the way you appear to the rest of the world and since we all have to mix with others, you can learn to make the very best of what Venus has to offer you.

One of the great complications in the past has always been trying to establish exactly what zodiac position Venus enjoyed when you were born because the planet is notoriously difficult to track. However, we have solved that problem by creating a table that is exclusive to your Sun sign, which you will find on the following page.

Establishing your Venus sign could not be easier. Just look up the year of your birth on the following page and you will see a sign of the zodiac. This was the sign that Venus occupied in the period covered by your sign in that year. If Venus occupied more than one sign during the period, this is indicated by the date on which the sign changed, and the name of the new sign. For instance, if you were born in 1950, Venus was in Taurus until the 27th June, after which time it was in Gemini. If you were born before 27th June your Venus sign is Taurus, if you were born on or after 27th June, your Venus sign is Gemini. Once you have established the position of Venus at the time of your birth, you can then look in the pages which follow to see how this has a bearing on your life as a whole.

1920 GEMINI / 25.6 CANCER / 18.7 LEO
1921 TAURUS / 8.7 GEMINI
1922 LEO / 15.7 VIRGO
1923 GEMINI / 10.7 CANCER
1924 CANCER
1925 CANCER / 4.7 LEO
1926 TAURUS / 28.6 GEMINI
1927 LEO / 8.7 VIRGO
1928 GEMINI / 24.6 CANCER / 18.7 LEO
1929 TAURUS / 8.7 GEMINI
1930 LEO / 15.7 VIRGO
1931 GEMINI / 10.7 CANCER
1932 CANCER
1933 CANCER / 4.7 LEO
1934 TAURUS / 27.6 GEMINI
1935 LEO / 8.7 VIRGO
1936 GEMINI / 24.6 CANCER / 17.7 LEO
1937 TAURUS / 8.7 GEMINI
1938 LEO / 14.7 VIRGO
1939 GEMINI / 9.7 CANCER
1940 CANCER / 13.7 GEMINI
1941 CANCER / 3.7 LEO
1942 TAURUS / 27.6 GEMINI
1943 LEO / 9.7 VIRGO
1944 GEMINI / 23.6 CANCER / 17.7 LEO
1945 TAURUS / 7.7 GEMINI
1946 LEO / 14.7 VIRGO
1947 GEMINI / 9.7 CANCER
1948 CANCER / 6.7 GEMINI
1949 CANCER / 2.7 LEO
1950 TAURUS / 27.6 GEMINI
1951 LEO / 9.7 VIRGO
1952 GEMINI / 23.6 CANCER / 17.7 LEO
1953 TAURUS / 7.7 GEMINI
1954 LEO / 13.7 VIRGO
1955 GEMINI / 8.7 CANCER
1956 CANCER / 29.6 GEMINI
1957 CANCER / 1.7 LEO
1958 TAURUS / 26.6 GEMINI
1959 LEO / 9.7 VIRGO
1960 CANCER / 16.7 LEO
1961 TAURUS / 7.7 GEMINI
1962 LEO / 13.7 VIRGO
1963 GEMINI / 8.7 CANCER
1964 CANCER / 22.6 GEMINI
1965 CANCER / 1.7 LEO
1966 TAURUS / 26.6 GEMINI
1967 LEO / 10.7 VIRGO
1968 CANCER / 16.7 LEO
1969 TAURUS / 6.7 GEMINI
1970 LEO / 13.7 VIRGO
1971 GEMINI / 7.7 CANCER
1972 CANCER / 22.6 GEMINI

1973 CANCER / 30.6 LEO
1974 TAURUS / 26.6 GEMINI / 22.7 CANCER
1975 LEO / 10.7 VIRGO
1976 CANCER / 15.7 LEO
1977 TAURUS / 6.7 GEMINI
1978 LEO / 12.7 VIRGO
1979 GEMINI / 7.7 CANCER
1980 CANCER / 22.6 GEMINI
1981 CANCER / 30.6 LEO
1982 TAURUS / 26.6 GEMINI / 21.7 CANCER
1983 LEO / 10.7 VIRGO
1984 CANCER / 15.7 LEO
1985 TAURUS / 6.7 GEMINI
1986 LEO / 12.7 VIRGO
1987 GEMINI / 6.7 CANCER
1988 CANCER / 22.6 GEMINI
1989 CANCER / 29.6 LEO
1990 TAURUS / 25.6 GEMINI / 20.7 CANCER
1991 LEO / 11.7 VIRGO
1992 CANCER / 14.7 LEO
1993 TAURUS / 5.7 GEMINI
1994 LEO / 11.7 VIRGO
1995 GEMINI / 5.7 CANCER
1996 CANCER / 22.6 GEMINI
1997 CANCER / 29.6 LEO
1998 TAURUS / 25.6 GEMINI / 20.7 CANCER
1999 LEO / 11.7 VIRGO
2000 CANCER / 14.7 LEO
2001 TAURUS / 5.7 GEMINI
2002 LEO / 11.7 VIRGO
2003 GEMINI / 5.7 CANCER
2004 CANCER / 22.6 GEMINI
2005 CANCER / 29.6 LEO
2006 TAURUS / 25.6 GEMINI / 20.7 CANCER
2007 LEO / 11.7 VIRGO
2008 CANCER / 14.7 LEO
2009 TAURUS / 5.7 GEMINI
2010 LEO / 11.7 VIRGO
2011 GEMINI / 5.7 CANCER
2012 CANCER / 22.6 GEMINI
2013 TAURUS / 25.6 GEMINI / 20.7 CANCER
2014 TAURUS / 25.6 GEMINI / 20.7 CANCER
2015 LEO / 11.7 VIRGO
2016 CANCER / 13.7 LEO
2017 TAURUS / 5.7 GEMINI
2018 LEO / 11.7 VIRGO

VENUS THROUGH THE ZODIAC SIGNS

Venus in Aries

Amongst other things, the position of Venus in Aries indicates a fondness for travel, music and all creative pursuits. Your nature tends to be affectionate and you would try not to create confusion or difficulty for others if it could be avoided. Many people with this planetary position have a great love of the theatre, and mental stimulation is of the greatest importance. Early romantic attachments are common with Venus in Aries, so it is very important to establish a genuine sense of romantic continuity. Early marriage is not recommended, especially if it is based on sympathy. You may give your heart a little too readily on occasions.

Venus in Taurus

You are capable of very deep feelings and your emotions tend to last for a very long time. This makes you a trusting partner and lover, whose constancy is second to none. In life you are precise and careful and always try to do things the right way. Although this means an ordered life, which you are comfortable with, it can also lead you to be rather too fussy for your own good. Despite your pleasant nature, you are very fixed in your opinions and quite able to speak your mind. Others are attracted to you and historical astrologers always quoted this position of Venus as being very fortunate in terms of marriage. However, if you find yourself involved in a failed relationship, it could take you a long time to trust again.

Venus in Gemini

As with all associations related to Gemini, you tend to be quite versatile, anxious for change and intelligent in your dealings with the world at large. You may gain money from more than one source but you are equally good at spending it. There is an inference here that you are a good communicator, via either the written or the spoken word, and you love to be in the company of interesting people. Always on the look-out for culture, you may also be very fond of music, and love to indulge the curious and cultured side of your nature. In romance you tend to have more than one relationship and could find yourself associated with someone who has previously been a friend or even a distant relative.

Venus in Cancer

You often stay close to home because you are very fond of family and enjoy many of your most treasured moments when you are with those you love. Being naturally sympathetic, you will always do anything you can to support those around you, even people you hardly know at all. This charitable side of your nature is your most noticeable trait and is one of the reasons why others are naturally so fond of you. Being receptive and in some cases even psychic, you can see through to the soul of most of those with whom you come into contact. You may not commence too many romantic attachments but when you do give your heart, it tends to be unconditionally.

Venus in Leo

It must become quickly obvious to almost anyone you meet that you are kind, sympathetic and yet determined enough to stand up for anyone or anything that is truly important to you. Bright and sunny, you warm the world with your natural enthusiasm and would rarely do anything to hurt those around you, or at least not intentionally. In romance you are ardent and sincere, though some may find your style just a little overpowering. Gains come through your contacts with other people and this could be especially true with regard to romance, for love and money often come hand in hand for those who were born with Venus in Leo. People claim to understand you, though you are more complex than you seem.

Venus in Virgo

Your nature could well be fairly quiet no matter what your Sun sign might be, though this fact often manifests itself as an inner peace and would not prevent you from being basically sociable. Some delays and even the odd disappointment in love cannot be ruled out with this planetary position, though it's a fact that you will usually find the happiness you look for in the end. Catapulting yourself into romantic entanglements that you know to be rather ill-advised is not sensible, and it would be better to wait before you committed yourself exclusively to any one person. It is the essence of your nature to serve the world at large and through doing so it is possible that you will attract money at some stage in your life.

Venus in Libra

Venus is very comfortable in Libra and bestows upon those people who have this planetary position a particular sort of kindness that is easy to recognise. This is a very good position for all sorts of friendships and also for romantic attachments that usually bring much joy into your life. Few individuals with Venus in Libra would avoid marriage and since you are capable of great depths of love, it is likely that you will find a contented personal life. You like to mix with people of integrity and intelligence but don't take kindly to scruffy surroundings or work that means getting your hands too dirty. Careful speculation, good business dealings and money through marriage all seem fairly likely.

Venus in Scorpio

You are quite open and tend to spend money quite freely, even on those occasions when you don't have very much. Although your intentions are always good, there are times when you get yourself in to the odd scrape and this can be particularly true when it comes to romance, which you may come to late or from a rather unexpected direction. Certainly you have the power to be happy and to make others contented on the way, but you find the odd stumbling block on your journey through life and it could seem that you have to work harder than those around you. As a result of this, you gain a much deeper understanding of the true value of personal happiness than many people ever do, and are likely to achieve true contentment in the end.

Venus in Sagittarius

You are lighthearted, cheerful and always able to see the funny side of any situation. These facts enhance your popularity, which is especially high with members of the opposite sex. You should never have to look too far to find romantic interest in your life, though it is just possible that you might be too willing to commit yourself before you are certain that the person in question is right for you. Part of the problem here extends to other areas of life too. The fact is that you like variety in everything and so can tire of situations that fail to offer it. All the same, if you choose wisely and learn to understand your restless side, then great happiness can be yours.

Venus in Capricorn

The most notable trait that comes from Venus in this position is that it makes you trustworthy and able to take on all sorts of responsibilities in life. People are instinctively fond of you and love you all the more because you are always ready to help those who are in any form of need. Social and business popularity can be yours and there is a magnetic quality to your nature that is particularly attractive in a romantic sense. Anyone who wants a partner for a lover, a spouse and a good friend too would almost certainly look in your direction. Constancy is the hallmark of your nature and unfaithfulness would go right against the grain. You might sometimes be a little too trusting.

Venus in Aquarius

This location of Venus offers a fondness for travel and a desire to try out something new at every possible opportunity. You are extremely easy to get along with and tend to have many friends from varied backgrounds, classes and inclinations. You like to live a distinct sort of life and gain a great deal from moving about, both in a career sense and with regard to your home. It is not out of the question that you could form a romantic attachment to someone who comes from far away or be attracted to a person of a distinctly artistic and original nature. What you cannot stand is jealousy, for you have friends of both sexes and would want to keep things that way.

Venus in Pisces

The first thing people tend to notice about you is your wonderful, warm smile. Being very charitable by nature you will do anything to help others, even if you don't know them well. Much of your life may be spent sorting out situations for other people, but it is very important to feel that you are living for yourself too. In the main, you remain cheerful, and tend to be quite attractive to members of the opposite sex. Where romantic attachments are concerned, you could be drawn to people who are significantly older or younger than yourself or to someone with a unique career or point of view. It might be best for you to avoid marrying whilst you are still very young.

CANCER:
2017 DIARY PAGES

2017

1 SUNDAY
Moon Age Day 11   Moon Sign Aquarius

There is a great urge on your part to get on well with others and to involve them more and more in your plans. You see well ahead of yourself in most situations and can afford to back your intuition. Some people might even call you psychic at the moment because it is so easy for you to assess how any particular situation will turn out.

2 MONDAY
Moon Age Day 12   Moon Sign Aquarius

Now is a really good time to be taking stock and to decide whether the direction you are taking in life is really what you want. Dump some of the baggage and make sure that you focus on priorities. It's too easy for Crabs to become fettered by an over-active sense of responsibility, sometimes on behalf of the whole world.

3 TUESDAY
Moon Age Day 13   Moon Sign Pisces

Personal and business encounters with others are likely to turn out quite favourably under present trends but beware because there are one or two people around who you won't get on with at all well. This might not be your fault but to avoid feelings of guilt later you should stay away from arguments with anyone today.

4 WEDNESDAY
Moon Age Day 14   Moon Sign Pisces

Certain situations demand a great deal of concentration today and you will be quite willing to put in that extra effort that means getting things right first time. It might seem as though you are somehow wasting valuable hours but in the longer-term it benefits you no end not to have to revisit situations more than once.

5 THURSDAY
Moon Age Day 15   Moon Sign Aries

Socially speaking there isn't any doubt that you are going to be in great demand – so much so that it might be awkward trying to do everything that is expected of you. You need to balance public obligations and personal desires, whilst at the same time finding moments during which you can reassure and help family members.

6 FRIDAY
Moon Age Day 16   Moon Sign Aries

It's time to prune parts of your life that are growing out of control – and in this way to allow the sun to shine in. October might seem a strange time for any sort of spring clean but that's what the planets are saying. There are times ahead that are going to demand your full attention and a less cluttered approach to life.

7 SATURDAY
Moon Age Day 17   Moon Sign Taurus

If others show themselves to have strong opinions today, yours are going to be stronger still. When friends or colleagues insist on arguing you can shout louder – though of course that is something you will avoid if you can. The simple fact is that you won't be put upon by anyone just now and will be quick to defend yourself.

8 SUNDAY
Moon Age Day 18   Moon Sign Taurus

You may feel that it would be sensible to simplify your life in some way – in fact in as many ways as you possibly can. Travelling light suits the Crab best, but instead you tend to insist on picking up baggage as you go along. Every so often dump some of the surplus load and boy will you feel better as a result.

9 MONDAY
Moon Age Day 19   Moon Sign Taurus

A personal attachment should prove to be very reassuring today and offers you the chance to say something that has been on your mind for a while. Don't try to crowd too many jobs into too short a time or you could end up doing everything badly. Take life one step at a time until tomorrow, when general trends are improving.

10 TUESDAY   *Moon Age Day 20*   *Moon Sign Gemini*

Be accommodating when it comes to the opinions of others and don't try to enforce your regimes on to people who are obviously reluctant. It's hard enough keeping your own life on track, without trying to do so for everyone else. Cancer could tend to be a little bossy at the moment and that's something to avoid.

11 WEDNESDAY   *Moon Age Day 21*   *Moon Sign Gemini*

A stimulating force is at work as you take a more expansive approach to life. Desire for the new and the unusual is especially strong at present and you will be moving heaven and earth in order to open up new avenues and exciting horizons. Why not opt for a long journey in the near future? The planets show it to be a good option.

12 THURSDAY   *Moon Age Day 22*   *Moon Sign Cancer*

This is an excellent day to start something new and to be in charge of your own destiny. Everything is likely to be working for you except the slight awareness that certain other people want to tell you how you should live your life. Make it quite plain, in your usual tactful way, that you know exactly what you want.

13 FRIDAY   *Moon Age Day 23*   *Moon Sign Cancer*

Today is definitely the best day of the month for capitalising on what stands around you at present. Pipe dreams have no real part to play in your world for the moment and you are quite prepared to look reality square in the face and to make it work for you. Gains can come from the most surprising places while you are so creative.

14 SATURDAY   *Moon Age Day 24*   *Moon Sign Leo*

You will still prefer to be mostly on the move today and can make this a special sort of Saturday. Getting involved in more than one major project is not only likely at the moment it's virtually mandatory. Nothing is too much trouble if you know that your efforts now are going to mean more of what you really want in the weeks to come.

15 SUNDAY   *Moon Age Day 25   Moon Sign Leo*

Maybe you should now be slightly less sensitive to what are, after all, the casual remarks of other people. It may seem as if these are directed at you but in reality you are simply over-analysing. Be cool, calm and collected in all situations and laugh off any setbacks because these are likely to be nothing to worry about.

16 MONDAY   *Moon Age Day 26   Moon Sign Virgo*

You are a zodiac sign with a natural talent for communication at the moment. Mercury is in a really good position in your chart and it should keep you chatting on throughout the whole day and beyond. You might even talk in your sleep, so keen are you at the moment to let people know how you really feel about everything.

17 TUESDAY   *Moon Age Day 27   Moon Sign Virgo*

Present relationships should be quite harmonious and there is a strong chance that romance will colour your attitudes and your day right now. At this stage of the week you are watching and waiting, anxious to co-operate at work and willing to compromise if necessary. New personalities could enter your life.

18 WEDNESDAY   *Moon Age Day 28   Moon Sign Libra*

The information you have been waiting for could arrive via your partner or someone to whom you are particularly close. Keep your eyes and ears open because it is possible to help yourself at every stage of today. Colleagues might be rather confused about something and it will be up to you to sort them out and to explain things fully.

19 THURSDAY   *Moon Age Day 29   Moon Sign Libra*

It could be necessary around now to sort out aspects of your life and to make sure that what is going on around you is what you really need. This may not be universally the case and some adjustments will be necessary. This is likely to be a practical sort of Thursday but there ought to be room for enjoyment too, most likely with your family.

20 FRIDAY
Moon Age Day 0   Moon Sign Libra

You may now desire to change your personal lifestyle – but do you have everything in place to make this possible? It is important to look at the details and to make sure everything is organised in the way you want it to be. Joint business matters will take up at least some of your time and the thought of financial gain is inspiring.

21 SATURDAY
Moon Age Day 1   Moon Sign Scorpio

It looks as though your personal life is in a period of transformation. It isn't that you are dumping relationships or insisting on changing everything for the sake of it. What is much more likely is that you are setting new trains in motion and then watching closely to see what happens. This evening brings strong social inclinations.

22 SUNDAY
Moon Age Day 2   Moon Sign Scorpio

Your need to analyse and to probe is stronger than ever and the fact that the Crab is so curious is putting you in potentially fortunate situations. You can answer questions that other people cannot and as a result colleagues and friends will be turning to you for advice. What matters the most now and what people notice is your originality.

23 MONDAY
Moon Age Day 3   Moon Sign Sagittarius

You generally have a good psychological understanding of your own nature and those of the people with whom you interact. This is especially true at the moment and it means you can quite easily second-guess the way they are likely to react under any given circumstance. Solving problems is likely to be quite straightforward now.

24 TUESDAY
Moon Age Day 4   Moon Sign Sagittarius

You should see that relationships are working out especially well at this stage of the week. At the same time you are entering a slightly dreamy phase for the next couple of days and you won't be half so motivated or physically inclined as you were. Learn that a great deal can also be gained from meditating and waiting in the wings.

25 WEDNESDAY   *Moon Age Day 5   Moon Sign Sagittarius*

You are gentle on yourself and also kind in the way you approach the world at large. This fact is not lost on others and although there will always be some people around who take advantage of your good nature, in the main this will not be the case. Get onside with colleagues who have ambitious plans and show your support.

26 THURSDAY   *Moon Age Day 6   Moon Sign Capricorn*

There is no sense in trying too hard today because you would simply be knocking your head against a brick wall. Let others take the strain while you sit back and enjoy the show. There is a tendency for you to stay close to home whenever possible and you are unlikely to start any new projects until the weekend.

27 FRIDAY   *Moon Age Day 7   Moon Sign Capricorn*

For once you could be showing quite poor people skills. This isn't like you at all but your accustomed intuition is now less evident than usual, as is your patience. You may not finish the working week on an excellent note but you will have kept your powder dry for later efforts. By the evening things should be looking better.

28 SATURDAY   *Moon Age Day 8   Moon Sign Aquarius*

You should prove to be both adventurous and optimistic this weekend and have what it takes to move the odd mountain if the desire to do so takes your fancy. You should also be quite physically motivated and even sporty. Whatever you decide to take on today is likely to turn out well because you have great determination.

29 SUNDAY   *Moon Age Day 9   Moon Sign Aquarius*

This is the ideal time to reflect for a little while on what has happened during October and how you can best use any good fortune that has come your way in order to get on better later. There should also be time for a good heart-to-heart with your partner or a family member who needs your support. Give advice but don't take over.

30 MONDAY
Moon Age Day 10   Moon Sign Pisces

The scope for personal freedom is strong and there are good rewards to be had from letting the world know that you are available and ready to take action. There are occasions when you are going to be rather forceful in the way you get your message across and that could shock those who are used to your quiet ways.

31 TUESDAY
Moon Age Day 11   Moon Sign Pisces

Your ego is strong and this could cause you the odd problem, although it also goes to prove how much you are enjoying life and how capable you actually are when it comes to getting things done. Not everyone wants to be your friend today but those people you care about are likely to adore you.

November
2017

1 WEDNESDAY   *Moon Age Day 12   Moon Sign Pisces*

Don't get too carried away today because although life looks exciting you also need to focus on what is really important. There are too many distractions around at present and these could cause you to miss something that could bring in more money and new options later. All it really takes is for you to keep your eyes and ears open.

2 THURSDAY   *Moon Age Day 13   Moon Sign Aries*

It is clear that you want to have fun and that you will also be keen to involve as many people as you can in some of your ingenious schemes. Not all of these might work out quite as intended but even if you only succeed in ten per cent you will end November somewhat better off than you began it.

3 FRIDAY   *Moon Age Day 14   Moon Sign Aries*

You really do need to feel useful today and will be doing all you can to be supportive of both colleagues and friends. Once the routine aspects of the day are dealt with the time will be right to have some fun. Involve family members if you can but it is especially important to make sure your partner plays a part in things.

4 SATURDAY   *Moon Age Day 15   Moon Sign Taurus*

The time seems right to tighten up certain securities – which ought to make you feel more comfortable with your life generally. Not everyone will have your best interests at heart right now but you show yourself to be shrewd and attentive, which means the chances of anyone duping you are as near to zero as makes no odds.

5 SUNDAY
Moon Age Day 16   Moon Sign Taurus

There isn't much doubt about your ability to get on extremely well with those people you care about the most but what might be even more important is your response to virtual strangers. A slight recent tendency to suspicion seems to be taking a holiday and you make new friends at every turn. One or two of these will prove to be significant.

6 MONDAY
Moon Age Day 17   Moon Sign Gemini

Today you strive for a peaceful and contented home-life. Whilst this is yours for the taking it is unlikely to be the end of the story because as soon as you sit down in your favourite chair you will become restless and will want to be on the move again. Relatives will think you must have ants in your pants.

7 TUESDAY
Moon Age Day 18   Moon Sign Gemini

If you want to make sure that everything you say is clearly understood you might have to make your position extremely clear. Don't worry that others will tire of hearing your voice. On the contrary you are going to be just about as popular as it is possible to be, whilst at the same time getting most of what you want from life.

8 WEDNESDAY
Moon Age Day 19   Moon Sign Cancer

You can now make the most of any career opportunities that are coming your way. It is important to pay attention because many benefits today will come like a bolt from the blue. This is the time of the month when you realise that life is not a rehearsal and that what you get out of it is directly related to what you have first put in.

9 THURSDAY
Moon Age Day 20   Moon Sign Cancer

You can rely on your personal charm to a great extent today and you should discover that good luck has more than a small part to play in your fortunes. This is because you are grabbing opportunities as they come along and you are wide awake to all of them. Friends should be extra supportive and really great to know now.

10 FRIDAY
Moon Age Day 21   Moon Sign Leo

If business or practical issues are up for discussion you are likely to be taking a leading role. You seem to have some really good ideas at the moment and will be quite happy to throw these in for what they are worth. Don't expect to make too much progress in matters of love today, through no fault of your own.

11 SATURDAY
Moon Age Day 22   Moon Sign Leo

With plenty of enjoyment in mind you are now less likely inclined than usual to be thinking about progress of any sort. The one exception might be a desire to do well in sporting activities. The Crab hates to be beaten and this facet of your nature is probably stronger now than would normally be the case.

12 SUNDAY
Moon Age Day 23   Moon Sign Virgo

What you hear from others today can contribute to the very progressive phase you are presently enjoying. The only slight fly in the ointment comes from colleagues or friends who promise more than they deliver. Keep on top of situations and if you realise that you can't rely on others, get cracking yourself. Your energy levels remain high.

13 MONDAY
Moon Age Day 24   Moon Sign Virgo

You simply want to achieve too much and as a result you might find that certain projects grind to a halt. Drop half of your expectations for the moment and concentrate on issues that are very nearly sorted. That way you will also find time for fun, which is probably more important than anything at this stage of November.

14 TUESDAY
Moon Age Day 25   Moon Sign Libra

You seem to have considerable charm at your disposal now and will be quite comfortable in situations that put you in the spotlight. This isn't always the case for the Crab but for the moment the shy side of your nature is definitely taking a holiday. Give some attention to progress at work whilst planetary assistance is at hand.

15 WEDNESDAY *Moon Age Day 26 Moon Sign Libra*

Your powers of concentration are especially good and will continue to be so throughout much of the rest of November. This means you can plan long-term and there is also a good chance that some of your efforts from earlier in the year now begin to bear fruit. It might be necessary to show your persuasive side today.

16 THURSDAY *Moon Age Day 27 Moon Sign Libra*

Work on business projects could be interesting, though there are times today when you will be quite happy to let others take the strain whilst you find newer and better ways to get things done. You are inspirational and will want to show an unsuspecting world that you can achieve a lot when left to get on with it.

17 FRIDAY *Moon Age Day 28 Moon Sign Scorpio*

A plan of action of any sort might need addressing and maybe altering, even before you have really got started. Actually that is the time to make changes because once things really get going you will be too occupied. The Crab is rarely as go-getting as it is at the present time so don't stand around waiting – get stuck in.

18 SATURDAY *Moon Age Day 0 Moon Sign Scorpio*

Intellectual and philosophical interests could be keeping you occupied as the weekend gets started. At the same time you will have itchy feet and might really enjoy a shopping spree with friends. Christmas isn't far away and there could be some real bargains to be had. You tend to spend very wisely at present.

19 SUNDAY *Moon Age Day 1 Moon Sign Sagittarius*

In a social sense there are a few ups and downs to deal with right now. You truly enjoy getting out there and doing new things. If circumstances hold you back or dictate that you are stuck in one place all the time a little frustration could be the result. This is a time to be in charge of your own destiny if at all possible.

20 MONDAY
Moon Age Day 2   Moon Sign Sagittarius

The way you approach your life at times ensures that you bring happiness to others, sometimes at the expense of your own desires. This is less likely to be true at present because you clearly have what it takes to make everyone else comfortable with their lives whilst at the same time finding contentment yourself.

21 TUESDAY
Moon Age Day 3   Moon Sign Sagittarius

Focus your energies on professional matters but learn to leave these alone once the working day is over. There is much more to your life than practical considerations, especially so under present planetary trends. New friendships are possible, together with an important realisation regarding a friend you already have.

22 WEDNESDAY
Moon Age Day 4   Moon Sign Capricorn

If you have any problem during the lunar low this month it will be that you tend to worry too much about details. For most Crabs the positive planetary trends are so good that the lunar low will pass virtually unnoticed. Now would be a good time to get on with those last-minute changes around the house ahead of the winter.

23 THURSDAY
Moon Age Day 5   Moon Sign Capricorn

Leave any major decisions until tomorrow – unless of course you have no choice. In situations where you can't delay you could do worse than to enlist the support and advice of a family member or good friend. Specialised jobs should be left to experts for the moment, or you could end up costing yourself money.

24 FRIDAY
Moon Age Day 6   Moon Sign Aquarius

There is likely to be a strong emphasis on both social and romantic possibilities as this particular working week draws towards its close. If you are looking for love you may choose to turn to methods you haven't tried before in order to meet the right person. All Cancerians will be extra warm and extremely kind under present trends.

61

25 SATURDAY   *Moon Age Day 7   Moon Sign Aquarius*

Nothing gets in the way of your intellectual curiosity at this time, even if you express it in a slightly quieter way than you occasionally do. You really do need to know why situations are the way they are and will be turning over all sorts of stones on the path of life simply so you can find out what's underneath.

26 SUNDAY   *Moon Age Day 8   Moon Sign Aquarius*

Success in most spheres of your life makes you feel fairly content with your lot, though it has to be said that you are also filled with burning desires that are not too easy to address or to achieve. It is so often the case that at the core of the Crab nature there is a divine discontent, often brought about because of slightly unrealistic expectations.

27 MONDAY   *Moon Age Day 9   Moon Sign Pisces*

This is likely to be another favourable time as far as your career is concerned. You know exactly how things ought to be going and will be doing all you can to alter circumstances to suit yourself. It won't be hard to get others involved in your schemes and it seems as if everyone wants to be on your team now.

28 TUESDAY   *Moon Age Day 10   Moon Sign Pisces*

Freedom is the key to happiness at present and there isn't much doubt that you will be at your best when you have hours in front of you to spend doing whatever takes your fancy. Not that you will be inclined to spend these alone. Your social motivation is strong and you will be keen to be involved in joyful events.

29 WEDNESDAY   *Moon Age Day 11   Moon Sign Aries*

Just discovering new possibilities could be pleasurable enough but right now you are taking things one stage further. You want to build on what you discover and to make everyone's life happier as a result. This might be a rather outlandish ambition but it is part of what makes you into the individual you are. Friends will be supportive now.

30 THURSDAY   *Moon Age Day 12   Moon Sign Aries*

Almost everything is working well for you as this most fortunate month draws to a close. The realisation that December is about to start could come as something of a shock, if only because you have been too busy to look at the calendar. Spend some time today listening carefully to the opinions of the people with whom you live.

December
2017

1 FRIDAY
Moon Age Day 13   Moon Sign Taurus

Whilst there doesn't seem to be much standing in your way today you could be subjected to the odd temperamental outburst by people who are clearly stressed. Do what you can to help them out, even if all you can manage is to have a chat with them. Your naturally sympathetic tendencies are definitely called into play right now.

2 SATURDAY
Moon Age Day 14   Moon Sign Taurus

It may have only just occurred to you that this is December and that means Christmas is only a stone's throw away. Don't use this fact as an excuse to panic because you probably have more sorted than you realise. In any case a degree of last-minute planning should make the festivities even more enjoyable for the Crab.

3 SUNDAY
☿ *Moon Age Day 15   Moon Sign Gemini*

When it comes to professional matters you now have such a persuasive manner that you could probably get more or less anything you want. Don't wait to be asked in any situation where it is clear to you that a specific action needs to be taken. By the time you have qualified your thoughts with someone else it might be too late.

4 MONDAY
☿ *Moon Age Day 16   Moon Sign Gemini*

Hold fire for a few hours and during the daylight hours be fairly circumspect in your actions. It isn't long before your confidence increases and there should be moments by this evening when the world really becomes your oyster. Plan now for what should be an eventful week ahead.

5 TUESDAY ☿ *Moon Age Day 17   Moon Sign Cancer*

Today signifies a period when just about anything could happen. Make an early start with all-important activities but don't do more than you have to in order to get the result you want in any particular situation. This would be a great day for a shopping spree or for travelling to see something you have been promising yourself for ages.

6 WEDNESDAY ☿ *Moon Age Day 18   Moon Sign Cancer*

You show yourself as being dynamic and even quite pushy in most matters today, which is a quite a departure for the Crab. As a result it might seem to some of your friends that they don't know you at all, which is why you have to make it obvious to them that you are as concerned, caring and cute as is usually the case.

7 THURSDAY ☿ *Moon Age Day 19   Moon Sign Leo*

This is exactly the right time of the month to take overall responsibility for your own ideas. If you insist on sharing everything with others, they will get the credit for something to which they have no right. The Crab isn't usually inclined to be selfish but there is a limit to generosity and if you stop to think about things you will realise you've reached it.

8 FRIDAY ☿ *Moon Age Day 20   Moon Sign Leo*

Communication with friends and colleagues is now likely to be quite stimulating. What's more it should also be highly productive. You do need to exercise a little care because it looks as though many Cancer people are burning the candle at both ends and in the middle too. A few minutes spent relaxing would do you the world of good.

9 SATURDAY ☿ *Moon Age Day 21   Moon Sign Virgo*

Don't go on today about things that are dead and gone in your life. You can only really prosper if you look ahead. Even though this is a naturally nostalgic time of the year there is no future in the past – either yours or anyone else's. If you are a little low today you can be sure the tendency will not last.

10 SUNDAY ☿ *Moon Age Day 22   Moon Sign Virgo*

You want to keep ahead of the field but that might be rather difficult to achieve on a Sunday. In any case this is not a good day during which to bring your work home with you. If you take some time out to maybe do a little shopping or to spend valuable hours with loved ones, you will be much more attentive and successful tomorrow.

11 MONDAY ☿ *Moon Age Day 23   Moon Sign Virgo*

Emotional matters could seem somewhat tense and extra effort is necessary if you want to sort out hiccups in relationships. This will only be possible if other people want to get involved and of course it takes two to tango. Away from the emotional arena you should find that financial matters are better than you thought.

12 TUESDAY ☿ *Moon Age Day 24   Moon Sign Libra*

Being the centre of attention isn't exactly difficult for you today. In amongst the start of the December festivities you could be put on some sort of pedestal – most likely by more than one person. You are at your very best in social situations and positively glow with good health and vitality. This is a good time for the Crab.

13 WEDNESDAY ☿ *Moon Age Day 25   Moon Sign Libra*

It could help today to pay attention to the finer details of life, especially where work is concerned. Others may not be keen on the way you present yourself but if you know it works – do it. You can't be flavour of the month with everyone at the moment but the people who think you are fantastic will show it all the time.

14 THURSDAY ☿ *Moon Age Day 26   Moon Sign Scorpio*

You should now be in a good position to organise yourself in practical matters. Professional headway is easier to achieve and there are new and better incentives waiting in the wings. This could also be a good day as far as romance is concerned as you are able to show your affection to a much greater extent.

15 FRIDAY ☿ *Moon Age Day 27 Moon Sign Scorpio*

Socially speaking you now have a definite thirst for freedom and excitement. It looks as though the Crab is developing the Christmas spirit well and this would not be particularly surprising because this is a time of year you relish. Join in the fun wherever you find it and arrange some sort of get-together if possible.

16 SATURDAY ☿ *Moon Age Day 28 Moon Sign Scorpio*

You can get your own way today primarily through your charm, which is always the greatest weapon in the Crab's armoury. You can put your talents to especially good use in a romantic setting and will be on form when it comes to exploiting newer and better ideas. At home romance begins to blossom.

17 SUNDAY ☿ *Moon Age Day 29 Moon Sign Sagittarius*

Some relationships may be on a hair trigger today, so take special care not to offer unintended offence to people who are too sensitive for their own good. This is less inclined to happen at home, where personal relationships are likely to be settled and happy. Friends may have a special need of you this evening.

18 MONDAY ☿ *Moon Age Day 0 Moon Sign Sagittarius*

Things keep moving forward for you under present astrological trends and there is no sign of life slowing down at any time now. On the contrary it looks as though you will be doing rather too much and that could mean fatigue unless you take care. Who knows where new possibilities will lead? Life should be very exciting.

19 TUESDAY ☿ *Moon Age Day 1 Moon Sign Capricorn*

Such is the state of play in your solar chart that your ambitions remain strong, even though you don't presently have the wherewithal to do anything about them. This can lead to a certain amount of frustration so be circumspect if you want to avoid getting in a state. Relax and meditate – that's the way forward.

20 WEDNESDAY ☿ *Moon Age Day 2   Moon Sign Capricorn*

The lunar low could continue to make you feel listless and lacking in any overall strategy. For this reason the Christmas tree may lose all its needles, the decorations will keep falling on your head and the children will be demanding presents you've never even heard of. What else can you do but sit down and laugh?

21 THURSDAY ☿ *Moon Age Day 3   Moon Sign Capricorn*

Getting your own way remains generally simple and is down to a combination of determination and your naturally winning ways. You just know that what you believe is right and when you have true conviction on your side you are unstoppable. Social moments could be quieter but might include a romantic interlude.

22 FRIDAY ☿ *Moon Age Day 4   Moon Sign Aquarius*

You seem to get the very best from communicating with others today. This is because you have what it takes to modify your own nature for the sake of those around you. Even the most difficult of individuals will once again fall prey to your charm and you can deal effectively with all practical matters. Do save time to be with your partner.

23 SATURDAY *Moon Age Day 5   Moon Sign Aquarius*

A fresh exchange of views would suit you fine today and you won't be at all insulted if someone wishes to modify one of your own initiatives. You are great when it comes to co-operation – even with people who have been difficult to deal with in the past. Niggling routines could get in the way of absolute enjoyment within your home.

24 SUNDAY *Moon Age Day 6   Moon Sign Pisces*

Your own ambitions are now particularly strong and they could get in the way of the wishes of people in your vicinity. That can't be helped because at the end of the day we all have to look out for number one. Christmas Eve brings a contented feeling that details have been dealt with but it's a pound to a penny you've forgotten something.

25 MONDAY
Moon Age Day 7   Moon Sign Pisces

On Christmas Day it turns out that all your efforts have been entirely worthwhile. Not that you seem to be universally appreciated but you can live with that. What does matter is that you manage to please someone who maybe hasn't enjoyed the best of years and it is this charitable side of your nature that makes you so loveable.

26 TUESDAY
Moon Age Day 8   Moon Sign Pisces

Spending time with loved ones is definitely to be recommended today. Not only do they give you the emotional support you always need but they can talk over shared experiences from the past that are presently contributing to your feelings about the future. This could turn out to be the quietest day across the Christmas holidays.

27 WEDNESDAY
Moon Age Day 9   Moon Sign Aries

Take care not to expect something from a friend that is going to be very difficult if not impossible for them to deliver. Maybe you are not thinking things through as clearly as you normally do or it could be that you are just slightly less sensitive. Look at matters carefully and leave room for flexibility.

28 THURSDAY
Moon Age Day 10   Moon Sign Aries

Any new social contacts will represent a marvellous tonic because just at the moment Cancer is as gregarious and sociable as it ever gets. Whilst others might get tired of the social whirl and demand a little rest, you will be dancing on until dawn. If anyone can make the best of the Christmas holidays it is certain that you will be one of them.

29 FRIDAY
Moon Age Day 11   Moon Sign Taurus

You have a talent for working hard and effectively and this really shows. Some Crabs will be back at work today and if you are one of them make certain that superiors know you are around. There is nothing at all wrong with singing your own praises a little, particularly since there is less competition around for the moment.

30 SATURDAY   *Moon Age Day 12   Moon Sign Taurus*

Although you continue to show your best and most organised face to the world you could stumble when you come across individuals who fail to respond to your charm. There are always going to be those who are immune to your delightful personality but in the rush to achieve every greater success you may simply have to ignore them.

31 SUNDAY   *Moon Age Day 13   Moon Sign Gemini*

It appears that your mind will be focused as much on the past as it is on the future and as long as you can achieve a sensible balance everything should be fine. By the end of today you will no doubt be reconciled to that same old New Year party or gathering but you could be quite surprised at the way things eventually pan out.

CANCER:
2018 DIARY PAGES

CANCER:
YOUR YEAR IN BRIEF

There are many gains to be had early this year, not least of all in a personal sense because for many Cancerians January and February proves to be very romantic. At the same time you are likely to be consolidating efforts from late last year to increase your finances significantly. Don't forget to show special regard at this time for a family member who is doing especially well in some way.

As the spring begins to show itself in the hedgerows, you grow more generally comfortable because you are a person who loves longer days and good weather. March and April should see you getting to grips with practicalities and especially keen to exercise. Money matters look particularly good towards the end of March and you are likely to find new enterprises waiting in the wings for you to embrace.

As May and June come along you might decide to make changes in and around your home, and with plenty of enthusiasm from family members this should be a fairly easy undertaking. Although you always have concern for those you love it is likely to be during May that you feel a greater family commitment. The following month of June increases these trends and also finds you anxious for change and diversity.

Avoid being too keen to overturn previous ideas as July gets started since there may be a little future in the past. Those around you have good ideas, many of which you will take on board. July turns out to be an excellent month for travel, as will be August. Establish a good balance between work and play. August will continue the good trends in romance, and may bring financial rewards.

In September and October your mood changes and there is a tendency to feel defeated before you start. This is not at all typical of the way you have been throughout most of the year and only serves to hold you back, so resist these feelings as strongly as possible. Increasing confidence should be noticeable as the autumn progresses, and October also brings better financial potential and an ability to see situations more clearly. Lady Luck may also pay you a visit as the weeks pass.

November could bring you closer to your heart's desire than at any other time throughout 2018 but you will have to work steadily and carefully towards your objectives. It looks almost certain that you will be making new friends, some of whom will stay around for many years. December is a busy month, partly because of Christmas, but should also see you finding new ways to have fun and taking great delight in outings and social events. Look towards the New Year with confidence and a belief in yourself.

January

2018

1 MONDAY
Moon Age Day 14   Moon Sign Gemini

Run of the mill responses to any question probably won't work on this New Year's Day and you will have to be quite original if you want people to remember you. That shouldn't be too difficult, and there is a good chance that a present run of good luck is likely to be maintained. If you are at work, expect some small anxiety in a professional relationship.

2 TUESDAY
Moon Age Day 15   Moon Sign Cancer

Today the Moon moves into your own zodiac sign of Cancer. This brings that part of the month known as the lunar high and marks a generally successful and enterprising period for you. People want to have you around because you contribute so much to whatever is taking place and you are likely to be luckier than is sometimes the case.

3 WEDNESDAY
Moon Age Day 16   Moon Sign Cancer

You are likely to be very creative in your thinking today and others will quite naturally follow your lead, probably without thinking too much about the situation. Getting to grips with thorny problems is easy and you move speedily from one task to the next. You will also be good at mixing business with pleasure under this trend.

4 THURSDAY
Moon Age Day 17   Moon Sign Leo

Things continue to improve and your natural ability to get on with just about anyone definitely works to your advantage around now. Anything that is attainable is completed in record time and even things you previously thought impossible could be within your reach. Someone else's bad luck could do you a good turn but don't feel bad about it.

5 FRIDAY
Moon Age Day 18   Moon Sign Leo

You remain quite energetic and should be willing to put yourself out for the sake of others at this time. Newer and better chances to get ahead in your career are there for the taking, even if it is difficult to recognise some of them at first. In a romantic mood, impressing your lover ought to be fairly easy.

6 SATURDAY
Moon Age Day 19   Moon Sign Virgo

You know what you like and you like what you see when it comes to your social life at this time. There are many different sorts of people around and you can get the very best from all of them. Not that you have to work hard in order to do so. Your personality means that people like you instinctively, which is a great advantage.

7 SUNDAY
Moon Age Day 20   Moon Sign Virgo

It should be plain sailing in terms of love and romance for you, with plenty of positive attention coming your way and with the chance for Crabs who are not emotionally attached to attract someone they see as being very special. Sadly, you should not be too hopeful about making a lot of money for the next few days.

8 MONDAY
Moon Age Day 21   Moon Sign Libra

Make this a day for doing whatever takes your fancy and if you can take a day off, do so. There are some domestic tasks that can be shelved for a while and this will leave you the time you need to enjoy yourself alongside people you really like. There is much laughter about now, most of it originating from you.

9 TUESDAY
Moon Age Day 22   Moon Sign Libra

What you feel like inside and the way you come across to the world at large can be two very different things under present trends. Even when you are shaking in your boots it will look to everyone around you as if you are confident and calm. It is now possible to move towards situations that have been blocked to you in the past.

10 WEDNESDAY   *Moon Age Day 23   Moon Sign Scorpio*

You might be on the last lap of a race that has occupied you for some time and whatever you decide to do at present, leave some time aside to reassess situations in the light of present evidence. Not everyone will behave as you have come to expect and that means having to change your own nature somewhat to suit circumstances.

11 THURSDAY   *Moon Age Day 24   Moon Sign Scorpio*

Out of complications come surprises and a realisation that you are cleverer than you thought yourself to be. Don't walk away from challenges today because these are the forges within which much success is created. One thing you won't relish at the moment is arguments – but then it isn't in your nature to be argumentative.

12 FRIDAY   *Moon Age Day 25   Moon Sign Scorpio*

The attitude of those around you could cause the odd difficulty and it may seem as though life is an uphill struggle in some ways. You have what it takes to show just how much you know and you should be socialising all the time. Don't get tied down with tasks you find either boring or absolutely pointless.

13 SATURDAY   *Moon Age Day 26   Moon Sign Sagittarius*

The way you express yourself is quite important on this particular Saturday. What you get now is directly proportional to the amount of effort you are willing to put in. Keep up with jobs that have been piling up at home but make them into a joy by enlisting the support of people you love to have around, especially cheerful types.

14 SUNDAY   *Moon Age Day 27   Moon Sign Sagittarius*

This is when you realise that life is not a rehearsal and that you will have to put in a lot of effort if you want your performance to draw the attention of the crowd. Superiors are likely to notice you if you are a weekend worker and that gives you an extra chance to impress, which could lead to a stronger financial base for the future.

15 MONDAY   *Moon Age Day 28   Moon Sign Capricorn*

Now the Moon moves into your opposite zodiac sign of Capricorn and brings the part of the month known as the lunar low. During this time you will be quieter, less likely to push yourself forward and more inclined to take valuable rest. Don't expect good luck until the middle of the week.

16 TUESDAY   *Moon Age Day 0   Moon Sign Capricorn*

You should be happy to look out at the world from inside your own shell and your quiet approach could confuse and even puzzle people who expect you to be lively and enterprising all the time. Be willing to allow subordinates or even family members to do things on your behalf and disguise this need on your part as delegation.

17 WEDNESDAY   *Moon Age Day 1   Moon Sign Capricorn*

There are rewards to be gained at home, especially in connection with family members. You are good at resolving arguments and you will be quite happy to play the honest broker away from home as well. Your finances look reasonably strong and you continue to make a favourable impression on just the right people.

18 THURSDAY   *Moon Age Day 2   Moon Sign Aquarius*

You may now consider reorganising your social life and while you are at it you could also be looking at personal attachments with new eyes. As usual you will be trying to do several different things at the same time but you have what it takes to manage all of them successfully. You can score some real firsts around this time.

19 FRIDAY   *Moon Age Day 3   Moon Sign Aquarius*

Today should be all about enjoying yourself, most likely in the company of people who have the same sense of fun that you possess. You have a good chance to learn something new and you would also be especially good at anything that requires co-ordination. You see through to the very heart of almost everything right now.

20 SATURDAY   *Moon Age Day 4   Moon Sign Pisces*

You could feel slightly held back from doing the things you really want to do, often by circumstances that appear to be beyond your own control. Instead of worrying about it, get on and start something new. The less fettered you feel by prevailing circumstances, the keener you will be to embark on new projects.

21 SUNDAY   *Moon Age Day 5   Moon Sign Pisces*

Take full advantage of domestic situations and all family gatherings and attachments. At this time of year you probably cannot be quite as social as you are in the warmer months but you can make the most of the personal possibilities that are offered to you. Stay warm but do try to get out when you can. Simply wrap yourself up well.

22 MONDAY   *Moon Age Day 6   Moon Sign Pisces*

Your love of life is quite in evidence today and so we find you starting the week in a very positive frame of mind. There is nobody more pleasant or good to have around than someone born under the sign of Cancer. You spread joy wherever you go and most important of all you are funny. This is the time to persuade people to follow you.

23 TUESDAY   *Moon Age Day 7   Moon Sign Aries*

Communication matters are well highlighted for you at the moment meaning that you can get more of what you want if you talk to other people. It isn't just a matter of persuading those around you to follow your lead because you also have a lot to learn from them. The chances are that you will chat happily to almost anyone today.

24 WEDNESDAY   *Moon Age Day 8   Moon Sign Aries*

You tend to express yourself at the moment through strong and vigorous feelings. There are no half-measures to your nature at this stage of the month and you are quite certain of all your facts. Just remember that there is still plenty you can learn – so listening to what others have to tell you is just as important as instructing them.

25 THURSDAY   *Moon Age Day 9   Moon Sign Taurus*

You really do need to be noticed at the moment and you won't be happy to be ignored. On a practical level, you need to keep specific, important issues in mind. You may be inclined to go off at a tangent, which isn't advisable under present trends. Seek the advice of an experienced professional if necessary.

26 FRIDAY   *Moon Age Day 10   Moon Sign Taurus*

This could be a time of minor change in your personal life. It is important at present to re-evaluate your goals and to lay your intentions out clearly, even if you have to write them down to fully understand them yourself. Friendships might bring a little inconvenience but that isn't much to ask in exchange for the happiness they also bring.

27 SATURDAY   *Moon Age Day 11   Moon Sign Gemini*

This is a time to enjoy comfortable chats with people you like. Even individuals who have not played a significant role in your life previously are now more likely to do so and you could get to know a stranger rather well during the next few days. Look for the odd or unusual in life and concentrate on trying to understand it.

28 SUNDAY   *Moon Age Day 12   Moon Sign Gemini*

You have a great enthusiasm for life today that is being inspired by others. Keep up your efforts to make a good impression, especially if you are at work, and don't leave any stone unturned when it comes to getting what you really want, particularly from professional matters. Your social instincts are very strong at this time, too.

29 MONDAY   *Moon Age Day 13   Moon Sign Cancer*

Today the Moon moves into your own zodiac sign of Cancer, bringing with it the second lunar high of January. For the next two or three days you are likely to throw caution to the wind and to go out to get what you really want most from life. Better luck attends you and you can afford to take a few calculated risks.

30 TUESDAY
Moon Age Day 14   Moon Sign Cancer

Make an early start today with new plans and pursue an idea wherever you have to go to follow it. Your nature at the moment is likely to be optimistic, cheerful and accommodating. Others will find you a joy to have around and you will even be more positive and decisive than is often the case for procrastinating Cancer.

31 WEDNESDAY
Moon Age Day 15   Moon Sign Leo

Professional life is a labour of love for you at the moment and you should be getting on very well in a financial sense too. As January draws to a close you will already be thinking about the spring and even the summer. Forward planning is well highlighted under present trends, especially so when it comes to any intention to travel.

February 2018

1 THURSDAY
Moon Age Day 16   Moon Sign Leo

You may have an opportunity to improve your domestic situation but you are unlikely to be moving any further from your home and family than necessary in order to achieve your objectives. You could be slightly socially reluctant but bear in mind that this is a trend that lasts for only a short time.

2 FRIDAY
Moon Age Day 17   Moon Sign Virgo

Now you should find yourself on a definite winning streak and you won't be at all tardy when it comes to pushing your luck as far as you can. It is said that we make much of our own luck in life and that's certainly the case for Cancer now. The attitude of your partner or family members might take some thinking about later today.

3 SATURDAY
Moon Age Day 18   Moon Sign Virgo

It is said that you learn something new every day and there is little doubt that versatility is your best aid at this time. Turn your mind in new directions at the drop of a hat and refuse to continue doing things in the same old way simply for the sake of convention. Your attitude now is light, bright and extremely attractive.

4 SUNDAY
Moon Age Day 19   Moon Sign Libra

Domestic matters could turn out to be rather tiresome and you would be better off concentrating more on your social life. Younger family members especially could be less than rewarding in their attitude and it may seem as though everyone you are close to is creating problems. Stay away from confrontation.

5 MONDAY
Moon Age Day 20   Moon Sign Libra

You can capitalise especially well on opportunities at work and you won't have any difficulty coming to terms with rearrangements or changes that come like a bolt from the blue. Because you are so flexible you could be called upon to do something very different when you are away from work, perhaps enlivening your social life.

6 TUESDAY
Moon Age Day 21   Moon Sign Libra

You will enjoy an even higher profile amongst your friends today than usual and you should do all you can on this particular Tuesday to get out and about as much as possible. Don't stay behind closed doors, even if the weather is horrible. The more you mix with others the greater are the number of rewards that are likely to be coming your way.

7 WEDNESDAY
Moon Age Day 22   Moon Sign Scorpio

This would be a really good time to get new ideas started, as well as a fine interlude for thinking through your intended strategies for the longer-term future. None of this is going to restrict you in any way and it looks as though you will be constantly on the move and more than happy to join in with social invitations coming your way.

8 THURSDAY
Moon Age Day 23   Moon Sign Scorpio

Expanding your intellectual horizons would be no bad thing and at this stage of the week there are all sorts of new possibilities beckoning you on. This is the Crab at its best and you should be quite keen to exercise your right for independence, though without ruffling any feathers on the way. Your reactions now are instinctive and positive.

9 FRIDAY
Moon Age Day 24   Moon Sign Sagittarius

This can be a day of demands and responsibilities but none of these should get in the way of having fun. What happens in a professional sense today could be important and it might seem as though there is a great deal at stake. All the same, you should stay relaxed and approach life in your usual cheerful way.

10 SATURDAY   *Moon Age Day 25   Moon Sign Sagittarius*

The sort of information that comes from others could prove to be invaluable in terms of your career and also with regard to your wider social life. You won't be in the least reserved when it comes to getting involved in a little gossip because you learn so much as well as adding to the chatter. People could underestimate you at this time.

11 SUNDAY   *Moon Age Day 26   Moon Sign Sagittarius*

Your love life could be the most rewarding area at the moment, partly because of your own positive attitude but also because so much romance is finding its way in your direction. For some Crabs there are new love interests in the offing but be careful not to allow jealousy to arise between some of your most ardent admirers.

12 MONDAY   *Moon Age Day 27   Moon Sign Capricorn*

Your recent successful touch with others now goes into something of a temporary decline, mainly thanks to the arrival of the lunar low. You won't have as much patience as would normally be the case and you may have to count to ten on a number of occasions. It might be best to stick to your own devices whenever possible today.

13 TUESDAY   *Moon Age Day 28   Moon Sign Capricorn*

Take as few chances as possible today and be especially careful not to speculate when there is no guarantee of a significant reward. The way you get on with relatives today proves that you are likely to be better off sticking close to home if possible, as the outside world can seem somehow threatening.

14 WEDNESDAY   *Moon Age Day 29   Moon Sign Aquarius*

Getting along with others really well might mean you hogging the limelight a little more than would usually be the case. You usually share only too well but you will do better for the moment if you are out there in the lead. Stand by for some really significant compliments and react to them with your usual modesty.

15 THURSDAY   *Moon Age Day 0   Moon Sign Aquarius*

The pace of life is likely to step up, especially if you are a working Crab. You remain energetic and inspirational, even if you are occasionally faced with people who are about as negative as it is possible to be. Giving the right sort of advice to friends should be easy but don't necessarily expect them to follow it.

16 FRIDAY   *Moon Age Day 1   Moon Sign Aquarius*

You will have the confidence to make the first move in all romantic clinches and you continue to be attractive and to inspire others. There are gains to be made today from simply being in the right place at the right time and it looks as though people at work are now more inclined to follow your lead.

17 SATURDAY   *Moon Age Day 2   Moon Sign Pisces*

In social matters you become even more willing to listen to what everyone else is saying and you will also be happy to let others have their head. Your ability to delegate is never bad but for the moment it is exemplary. When it comes to negotiating a contract, or making a pact, be as honest and open as your wonderful nature makes possible.

18 SUNDAY   *Moon Age Day 3   Moon Sign Pisces*

One of your greatest talents is your ability to tune into the deepest emotional signals coming from loved ones, in fact, coming from almost anyone you encounter today. You read those around you as if they were open books and though this is definitely a gift, it can be quite unnerving to some people if you surprise them too much with your insight.

19 MONDAY   *Moon Age Day 4   Moon Sign Aries*

Your general good cheer at the moment enhances your social life and may intensify romantic relationships. Take care not to get sentiment mixed up with genuine affection, though. Looking after your friends is always second nature for you and right now you will do all you can for them.

20 TUESDAY   *Moon Age Day 5   Moon Sign Aries*

You want to be out and about and having as much fun as possible around now. Don't wait to be asked if there is something you really want to do. Today you are making the most of the running and you show everyone just what a fun-loving and easy-going sort of an individual the average Crab actually is.

21 WEDNESDAY   *Moon Age Day 6   Moon Sign Taurus*

Whatever you want today, you can proceed towards it with very little difficulty and plenty of enthusiasm. There are gains coming your way from all sorts of directions, some of which may be unexpected. It may not be usual for you to seize the initiative, but your present ability to do so is very much enhanced.

22 THURSDAY   *Moon Age Day 7   Moon Sign Taurus*

There could be strong resistance to some of your views today. Treat this as a sort of test. If you lose your temper as a result, then clearly you have failed. What you should be striving to achieve is a state of affairs in which you can use your kind nature to talk others round to your own attitude. That's a piece of cake to you!

23 FRIDAY   *Moon Age Day 8   Moon Sign Taurus*

Things are looking good and you seem to be keeping up quite a high profile on the social scene. This means that you are much in demand and could find the practical necessities of life getting in the way. Trying to achieve a state of balance is rarely difficult for you and there are times today when your nature shines out like the sun.

24 SATURDAY   *Moon Age Day 9   Moon Sign Gemini*

Life is fascinating and there is plenty of interest going on around you now. The only difficulty is that you can't be part of it all. Some patience is necessary, together with a need to prioritise. Getting ahead of yourself with tasks at home is likely to leave you more relaxation time during the days ahead.

25 SUNDAY
Moon Age Day 10   Moon Sign Gemini

The most rewarding times you experience today come from home and matters associated with personal relationships. Not everyone comes round to your way of thinking but you clearly have a silver tongue right now and should be able to get what you want most of the time. Friends could be quite demanding.

26 MONDAY
Moon Age Day 11   Moon Sign Cancer

A change of planetary emphasis now brings along a much more positive phase and the return of the go-getting individual you have naturally been over the last few weeks. Be prepared to act swiftly while the lunar high is around and don't wait to be invited to do anything that you know will improve your life.

27 TUESDAY
Moon Age Day 12   Moon Sign Cancer

All matters are positively helped by the position of the Moon right now and you will be more than able to assist others as you make your own way through life today. Much of what you choose do is as a result of instinct, together with a good dose of common sense. You should be quite energetic and more than willing to take the odd, calculated risk.

28 WEDNESDAY
Moon Age Day 13   Moon Sign Leo

A little caution may be necessary because it appears to others that you are only concerned with your own ideas right now. In a sense that is true, if only because you know you are correct in your general judgements. Get ahead with tasks you don't like, leaving yourself more time later in the day to do what you really want.

March

2018

1 THURSDAY
Moon Age Day 14   Moon Sign Leo

You could be slightly uncomfortable in social situations today and will be more inclined to keep your own counsel if at all possible. It isn't that you are opposed to being in company – but you could be somewhat happier to work on your own. In quiet moments your mind is more focused than ever.

2 FRIDAY
Moon Age Day 15   Moon Sign Virgo

Your love life should have an exciting element about it and the general power of your personality is so strong that people will marvel at your present intensity. The only fly in the ointment is that your usual sense of humour is lacking and you won't be quite as inclined to laugh at your own folly as usual.

3 SATURDAY
Moon Age Day 16   Moon Sign Virgo

Expect a rather tense day in terms of relationships, though this need not be a bad thing if you monitor situations carefully. It's true that you might be slightly on edge at the moment but that makes you more reactive and better placed to seize instant opportunities. Don't get too tied down with petty worries about things that are not important.

4 SUNDAY
Moon Age Day 17   Moon Sign Libra

You have a remarkable talent for dealing with people on all sorts of levels and this really shows itself under present trends. It doesn't matter whether you are talking to people at the bus stop or involving yourself in important business deals. What does matter today is that everyone is willing to listen to the voice of reason you represent.

5 MONDAY
Moon Age Day 18   Moon Sign Libra

You can now get the optimum from your working life and will show yourself in a very positive light when you are amongst people. In most situations you have what it takes to be in the lead and people should naturally defer to your opinions and wisdom. Expect a few small niggles today related to finances.

6 TUESDAY
Moon Age Day 19   Moon Sign Scorpio

Work opportunities that come along around now can lead to advancement. It isn't out of the question that some Crabs will even be thinking about a change in career, or at the very least a move within the same organisation. You may be looking for a situation that leaves more time to enjoy your family life and with some careful thought this could be possible.

7 WEDNESDAY
Moon Age Day 20   Moon Sign Scorpio

An instinctive sense of harmony pervades your life and you will now know automatically what looks and feels just right. In discussions you see both sides of all issues and you can be relied upon to be fair and unbiased when people require advice. This should be a strongly socially motivated sort of midweek period.

8 THURSDAY
Moon Age Day 21   Moon Sign Sagittarius

Professionally speaking you are now at a peak and there are plenty of opportunities for success – many coming like a bolt from the blue. Actually there is nothing at all strange about what is going on because when you stop to think about things you will realise it is your wise past actions that are leading to the gains that are on offer now.

9 FRIDAY
Moon Age Day 22   Moon Sign Sagittarius

Any sort of partnership should work out well for you at this time and you have what it takes to co-operate fully and to make new friends on the way. Even strangers are going to warm to your personality at this time and your close relationships help you to make the best of yourself. The Crab also shows its concern for others now.

10 SATURDAY   *Moon Age Day 23   Moon Sign Sagittarius*

Your personal relationships should now be steady and very rewarding, but the atmosphere with professional acquaintances might be slightly strained. It becomes obvious that you need to get your own way, which is so rare for Cancer that it shocks people. As is so often the case, diplomacy is the way forward.

11 SUNDAY   *Moon Age Day 24   Moon Sign Capricorn*

Don't make any concrete decisions today or tomorrow, or at least if you do make certain that you understand the implications of what you are taking on. If there are any small flaws in your thinking at present the lunar low is likely to expose them and extra care will be necessary when you are dealing with fragile relationships and family ties.

12 MONDAY   *Moon Age Day 25   Moon Sign Capricorn*

You could encounter some obstacles today which limit your progress – which is why it would be sensible to avoid doing more than you have to. Let others take the strain while you sit back and have a well-earned rest. Thinking time is essential for everyone and is especially important to the Crab at the moment. Be slow and steady today.

13 TUESDAY   *Moon Age Day 26   Moon Sign Aquarius*

You now have the opportunity to make agreements that are based on shared ideals and mutual benefits. This makes co-operation with others a dream and decisions you make today can have a positive bearing on what comes along months down the line. You may be expected to shine in a social setting and in this you won't let anyone down.

14 WEDNESDAY   *Moon Age Day 27   Moon Sign Aquarius*

Now only will you be put in positions that make you the centre of attention – you will actively seek them out. Although you may carefully rehearse what you have to say when you are in social settings, in the end you make it all up as you go along. That is the present gift of the Crab nature and is a gift worth having.

15 THURSDAY *Moon Age Day 28 Moon Sign Aquarius*

You may now discover people who are far more important to your life and success than you might have estimated even a week or two ago. The most unlikely individuals have it within their power to offer you timely assistance and you won't hang back when it comes to public speaking. All in all you should be on top form around now.

16 FRIDAY *Moon Age Day 29 Moon Sign Pisces*

Now you want to have as many facts and figures at your fingertips as you can manage to find. You won't be taking too many chances, especially when it comes to money, and you seem to know instinctively when to move and when it would be best to remain where you are. A few domestic routines could appeal to you.

17 SATURDAY *Moon Age Day 0 Moon Sign Pisces*

Most communication or travel matters should prove to be a joy today. You won't have any trouble at all making others understand what you are trying to tell them and you will be filled with enthusiasm for any new projects that crop up. Most important of all, you are willing to co-operate and so can gain from a group view of life.

18 SUNDAY *Moon Age Day 1 Moon Sign Aries*

When it comes to your general life you can now enjoy the feeling that you are more in command than you have been for quite some time. Whilst those around you tend to be too capricious for their own good, you move forward slowly and steadily towards your chosen objectives. Partnerships are especially important at this time.

19 MONDAY *Moon Age Day 2 Moon Sign Aries*

There are some gains to be made at the start of this week, mainly as a result of new ideas that are coming from a host of different directions. With everything to play for at work you should be making a good impression and you certainly won't be short of support when you need it the most. Romance also looks good this week.

20 TUESDAY
Moon Age Day 3   Moon Sign Aries

Work issues should be coming together quite nicely and this might actually be the most important area for you at this time. It may be that your true worth is being recognised much more than it was in the past. At the same time, you won't be keen to soldier on with tasks that bore you or which hold no fascination.

21 WEDNESDAY
Moon Age Day 4   Moon Sign Taurus

This is a great time to be throwing yourself into hard physical work of one sort or another. You have plenty of energy at the moment and could easily become bored with routines. The more you push yourself, the greater will be the feelings of satisfaction when you achieve your objectives. New horizons beckon at work.

22 THURSDAY
Moon Age Day 5   Moon Sign Taurus

Do what you can to build upon recent successes but don't be disheartened if you find that something you had planned will have to be thought out again. It is far better to get things right first time and it would definitely not be a good idea to rush into anything as this could lead the people you most need help from to doubt you.

23 FRIDAY
☿ *Moon Age Day 6   Moon Sign Gemini*

You could discover that information coming in from associates or even friends will be invaluable when it comes to organising or reorganising your life in some way. There is always more than one point of view so you should be quite circumspect before you embrace your own first notions fully. The time has come to take stock.

24 SATURDAY
☿ *Moon Age Day 7   Moon Sign Gemini*

You will need a little peace and quiet if you are to function perfectly today. With the Moon in your solar twelfth house there is a more of a tendency for you to retreat into yourself but this is only a temporary situation and won't last long. Nevertheless it is a useful period and ensures that your planning is sound.

25 SUNDAY   ☿   *Moon Age Day 8   Moon Sign Cancer*

Good luck is now much more likely to be on your side than it was over the last two or three days. It isn't that you are doing anything very differently, merely that you have what it takes to be in the right place at the right time to make gains. When it comes to your personal popularity, things could hardly be better.

26 MONDAY   ☿   *Moon Age Day 9   Moon Sign Cancer*

There are leadership issues to be sorted out today and since you are so assertive at the moment it is natural that people will turn to you for guidance. Whether you are likely to be comfortable in this role beyond the next couple of days remains to be seen but for the moment you are the general and the army wants to follow your lead.

27 TUESDAY   ☿   *Moon Age Day 10   Moon Sign Leo*

You could so easily find yourself at odds with someone close to you – maybe even a person you normally get on with extremely well. Either you might be grumpy or they are, but either way it takes two to tango. If you refuse to get involved in disagreements, they can't even take place. Remove yourself from situations that point to conflict.

28 WEDNESDAY ☿   *Moon Age Day 11   Moon Sign Leo*

Practical affairs should be more than fulfilling during the middle of this week and in fact they are likely to be the most important factors in your life for a day or two. It isn't that things are going wrong anywhere else, it's just that you want to concentrate on getting things done. The more you finish now, the sooner you will be starting something new.

29 THURSDAY   ☿   *Moon Age Day 12   Moon Sign Virgo*

Since things seem to be going fairly well on a material level, most other aspects of your life are likely to fall into place of their own accord. All the same, don't settle for too little and have some deep realisation of how hard you have worked in the past and what you are actually worth. Some excitement in your personal life could provide a welcome diversion now.

30 FRIDAY ☿ *Moon Age Day 13   Moon Sign Virgo*

Communication with certain other people could seem rather confused today, though this is not likely to be the case with your partner. Romance is one area of life that looks especially good around now and you may want to think up a really good gesture to deepen your lover's commitment to you. That won't be hard for you at present.

31 SATURDAY ☿ *Moon Age Day 14   Moon Sign Libra*

Trends move on and there is now a positive emphasis on communication today. Conversations with others provide the key to understanding your own motivations. Listen to the advice of someone older or wiser and also be willing to discuss things with family members. A casual relationship could quite soon turn into something a great deal more.

April 2018

1 SUNDAY ☿ Moon Age Day 15 Moon Sign Libra

Trials and tribulations could crop up unexpectedly today, probably at home, and most areas of responsibility could seem to be harder going than of late. The secret is probably not to get too involved in matters that are not your direct responsibility. Leave people to their own devices and don't offer any unsolicited advice now.

2 MONDAY ☿ Moon Age Day 16 Moon Sign Scorpio

This is a time when new partnerships may begin and you should be feeling very optimistic about co-operation of all sorts this week. Socially speaking you are likely to be in a freewheeling mood and you will also be more inclined to travel under present trends. If there are any frustrations today they should be small ones.

3 TUESDAY ☿ Moon Age Day 17 Moon Sign Scorpio

A sense of frustration can result from ego clashes that take place around now. It is most unlike you to be involved in such situations but if you feel you are right about anything today you are much more likely to argue the point than you normally would. Smooth out areas of friction by putting in responsible effort.

4 WEDNESDAY ☿ Moon Age Day 18 Moon Sign Scorpio

Personality clashes can take place when you are dealing with the practical side of life, so be as flexible as possible when you are dealing with people who seem determined to be awkward. It won't help to lose your temper because that will only lead to further complications. Better by far to count to ten.

5 THURSDAY ☿ *Moon Age Day 19 Moon Sign Sagittarius*

Your social life can now be especially rewarding and with new opportunities constantly coming your way you should enjoy this particular Thursday a great deal. The only thing you probably should not do is to stay locked away at home because if you do many of the possibilities of the day will be lost. It's important to move around.

6 FRIDAY ☿ *Moon Age Day 20 Moon Sign Sagittarius*

Today you really do need to be part of a group and you can draw inspiration from the ideas of colleagues or friends. The only slight problem is that you are also feeling quite independent in some ways and so won't always respond positively to be being told anything. It's really just a matter of being as flexible as the planets allow right now.

7 SATURDAY ☿ *Moon Age Day 21 Moon Sign Capricorn*

A little confusion and tiredness is now possible and you will be quite happy to take a break at the start of this weekend. As long as you don't overburden yourself there is no reason why the lunar low should have any real bearing on your life during April. What you do need is variety, at least in terms of the way you look at the future.

8 SUNDAY ☿ *Moon Age Day 22 Moon Sign Capricorn*

It is possible that you will miss certain appointments or be fairly absent minded whilst the Moon is in its present position but this is to be expected and should not be a major source of frustration. People might seem to avoid you but if they do it is probably only because you have put up a 'do not disturb' sign, without even realising that you have done so.

9 MONDAY ☿ *Moon Age Day 23 Moon Sign Capricorn*

It's true that you are very sensitive at the moment and you may even withdraw from situations you see as being confrontational or unpleasant. You want everything to be warm and cuddly at present and if you can't have it that way you might take your bat and go home. Avoid getting annoyed about little things you can't alter.

10 TUESDAY ☿ *Moon Age Day 24   Moon Sign Aquarius*

The Crab now has a bright, quick mind that makes you able to appreciate things in a flash. Looking at the big picture of life should be quite easy under present trends and you won't be at all put off by the prospect of major changes taking place. On the contrary it will be you that inspires many of them.

11 WEDNESDAY ☿ *Moon Age Day 25   Moon Sign Aquarius*

You could be at loggerheads in a particular relationship and you may face criticism as a result. Try to rise above your emotions and to look at situations impartially. This is a period that can offer many social possibilities and one in which fun may come along at the slightest invitation.

12 THURSDAY ☿ *Moon Age Day 26   Moon Sign Pisces*

Domestic family relationships could prove to be more rewarding today than those outside the home. The exception to this rule could be one special friend, to whom you will be extremely close at the moment. At work avoid getting hung up on details and spend time looking at the bigger picture.

13 FRIDAY ☿ *Moon Age Day 27   Moon Sign Pisces*

You can probably enjoy more leisure time now and much of the satisfaction you encounter comes from your inspirational nature. Doing things in different ways is something the Crab really needs and can be especially significant under present trends. All the same, a little realism is also called for.

14 SATURDAY ☿ *Moon Age Day 28   Moon Sign Pisces*

Everything should be reasonably easy-going and plain sailing on the relationship front and this is especially true for those Crabs who enjoy a stable, long-term attachment. At home you will be thinking up new ways to change your environment to better suit your needs and this should be a very family-led but quite enjoyable day.

15 SUNDAY   *Moon Age Day 29   Moon Sign Aries*

Mental inspiration can come from travel and from seeing old things in a new and quite revolutionary way. Your mind is open to new stimulus and you should be quite prepared to mix and match in terms of situations and people who are only now entering your life. The more variety that is possible, the greater is the satisfaction.

16 MONDAY   *Moon Age Day 0   Moon Sign Aries*

Anything new is likely to seem more interesting to you at the moment than going over old ground. Be careful what you do abandon though because you could lose out as a result. What you really need is a compromise between past efforts and new ideas. The Crab needs a really balanced approach today.

17 TUESDAY   *Moon Age Day 1   Moon Sign Taurus*

Current planetary trends may help you discover the right direction to take, especially in a personal sense. A positive attitude can take you a long way this week, and you need to be as open to change as possible. Try to do something new because you will be happiest when you are occupied and learning new skills.

18 WEDNESDAY   *Moon Age Day 2   Moon Sign Taurus*

You just love to have a good chat at the moment and you won't be fussy about who you talk to. This tendency makes you very attractive and you can turn on the charm any time you want. Gaining your objectives therefore becomes easier and there is less tension around than might have been the case earlier in the month.

19 THURSDAY   *Moon Age Day 3   Moon Sign Gemini*

You should be much more in the social mainstream now but there seems to be a great deal of ego about when it comes to personal attachments. Keep it light and easy-going today and avoid getting yourself involved in deep or philosophical discussions. Your soothing Crab charm can come in handy.

20 FRIDAY　　　*Moon Age Day 4　　Moon Sign Gemini*

With the Moon occupying your solar twelfth house today you could find yourself going through a fairly quiet interlude. This won't last long because things really get moving tomorrow but it could be useful to have some space and time to think. Friends may notice your contemplative attitude but let them know you are feeling fine.

21 SATURDAY　　　*Moon Age Day 5　　Moon Sign Cancer*

Now you can make up your own mind about virtually anything. You will also be making your own luck because you know instinctively how to be in the right place at the right time to get ahead. Golden opportunities for success come your way across the next couple of days and it's simply a matter of jumping on board the train.

22 SUNDAY　　　*Moon Age Day 6　　Moon Sign Cancer*

You can maximise the possibility of success now that the wheels of progress are turning ever faster. Being part of almost anything that is taking place around you is one way to keep up with events and at the same time you are so popular in a social sense that everyone wants you to be part of their immediate circle.

23 MONDAY　　　*Moon Age Day 7　　Moon Sign Leo*

Look out for slight difficulties in emotional attachments and treat these as being of concern but not paramount. What's happening here is that you are making adjustments but not everyone wants to come to terms with them. You won't be exactly awkward today but you will want people to listen to you.

24 TUESDAY　　　*Moon Age Day 8　　Moon Sign Leo*

You seem to thrive on a certain amount of change now. This is a time when you need to uproot and move yourself in some way – though you probably have no real idea how to go about it. You may not even be aware why you are feeling restless but everything should become clearer as the days pass.

25 WEDNESDAY   *Moon Age Day 9   Moon Sign Virgo*

Whilst you should not allow minor distractions to get in the way of your forward progress you might be stopping and starting quite a lot for the next day or two. This can lead to a certain amount of low-key frustration but won't hold you up too much. Friends should be very supportive at the moment and actively move to help you.

26 THURSDAY   *Moon Age Day 10   Moon Sign Virgo*

Relationships can give you pause for thought and your partner might be acting in a less than typical manner. Your own attitude might be the reason, especially if you seem to have been particularly restless recently. Your confidence can sometimes be lacking when you need it the most but you can help yourself by remaining positive.

27 FRIDAY   *Moon Age Day 11   Moon Sign Virgo*

Professional and business interests are likely to take second place to your personal life at the end of this week. You are anxious to make a good impression on your partner and to show how concerned you are for their well-being. A few small gestures and a simple 'I love you' could be all that's required.

28 SATURDAY   *Moon Age Day 12   Moon Sign Libra*

Along comes a planetary phase during which you are likely to put others first. There's nothing especially strange about this for Cancer but you are likely to be even more giving and concerned for the world than usual. Have patience with a particular job that you feel you are taking ages to complete.

29 SUNDAY   *Moon Age Day 13   Moon Sign Libra*

You can now move ahead and make even more progress, though what direction you choose to take seems to be entirely up to you. Friends are gathering around, or at least that's the way it seems, and your social hours are likely to be full and happy. If you can't get exactly what you want in a financial sense you need to be patient.

30 MONDAY

Moon Age Day 14   Moon Sign Scorpio

Your curious nature is really on display today and that turns you into a supreme communicator. You want to know what makes everything tick and will be more than happy to ask as many questions as necessary in order to find out. On the way you could meet some very interesting people and maybe even make new friends.

 *May* 2018

1 TUESDAY

Moon Age Day 15   Moon Sign Scorpio

This could be a very good time for pleasure trips and for having fun in the company of people who have a very similar outlook on life to your own. You are adventurous enough to try almost anything at the moment, but a little care may be necessary where your physical safety is concerned.

2 WEDNESDAY

Moon Age Day 16   Moon Sign Sagittarius

High spirits should be prevailing, especially in relationships, and your mood is almost certain to attract others. Look out for romantic interests, even if you have not been particularly motivated by them recently. People love to have you around and may go to extraordinary lengths to make you happy.

3 THURSDAY

Moon Age Day 17   Moon Sign Sagittarius

A time of clear insight when things should fall neatly into place, at least in your mind. Converting your thoughts into real situations could be rather more difficult but with good will all round there are gains to be made. Today is especially good for social gatherings and for travelling.

4 FRIDAY

Moon Age Day 18   Moon Sign Sagittarius

It won't have escaped your attention that the nights are getting lighter and the weather warmer. You are by nature a free spirit and you love to be outdoors whenever possible. If there is any spare time today spend it in the garden or walking in a local park. Just as surely as the flowers are growing so is your confidence and optimism.

5 SATURDAY   *Moon Age Day 19   Moon Sign Capricorn*

Things may not be going entirely your way at the start of this particular weekend. It's somewhat unfortunate having the lunar low around on a Saturday but it should not prevent you from prospering in small ways. What you may notice is that any real forward progress is restricted and people generally could seem awkward.

6 SUNDAY   *Moon Age Day 20   Moon Sign Capricorn*

You may lack the capacity to concentrate on any one subject and you will probably be happier allowing others to take the strain for the moment. That doesn't mean you fail to make any sort of progress, even if you do feel that you are taking one step forward and two back. Fall back on your sense of humour.

7 MONDAY   *Moon Age Day 21   Moon Sign Aquarius*

Continue to seek change and variety, if only for its own sake. New stimulus may be required if you want to achieve real happiness but there may be minor obstacles to overcome, especially at home. It ought to be possible to rely on the good offices of friends and you can also be sure of the support coming from your partner.

8 TUESDAY   *Moon Age Day 22   Moon Sign Aquarius*

Some tension could be accumulating, possibly at home but it could just as easily be in the workplace. Release comes from unexpected and sudden bursts of temper that are most unlike you. Hopefully, people will forgive the odd harsh word and luckily this trend won't last long. Spare some time to help a friend with problems now.

9 WEDNESDAY   *Moon Age Day 23   Moon Sign Aquarius*

Concentrate on what seems most important but leave time aside for having fun. You can't expect to be achieving something concrete all the time and in any case, you are inspired by the most random situations. What matters the most is that you are really paying attention, which is why you pick up on so many opportunities today.

10 THURSDAY · · · · · · · *Moon Age Day 24 · Moon Sign Pisces*

Understanding the importance of charm is absolutely essential to the Crab nature. You get what you want from life using your personality and not by stamping on anyone as you pass along life's road. This means you rarely make enemies and today shows just how willing everyone is to lend you a hand when you need it.

11 FRIDAY · · · · · · · · *Moon Age Day 25 · Moon Sign Pisces*

Attending to a variety of interests now allows you to get the very most from your life. This is likely to be a very busy phase and one during which you will be fully committed to everything that is exciting and inspirational. You should also be very creative, so perhaps consider some changes to your living space.

12 SATURDAY · · · · · · · *Moon Age Day 26 · Moon Sign Aries*

Friendships can be slightly spoiled today by suppressed tensions, though probably not on your part. All the same you might have to deal with people who are unruly or awkward and as a result you might be more comfortable amongst trusted family members. Take heart from the fact that this is a short trend and everything should seem different by tomorrow.

13 SUNDAY · · · · · · · · *Moon Age Day 27 · Moon Sign Aries*

If you can't impose your will on others then leave well enough alone. This is not a time to interfere in the affairs of others, especially since there are important issues of your own to deal with. Some surprises could come along later in the day and it is likely that you will be up for some kind of social challenge.

14 MONDAY · · · · · · · · *Moon Age Day 28 · Moon Sign Taurus*

You get along with others famously, and especially so under present planetary trends. This is of use to you in a number of different ways. Not only does your popularity make your social life more interesting, it also speeds up the emotional responses of others and makes for a better than average period as far as romance is concerned.

15 TUESDAY
Moon Age Day 0   Moon Sign Taurus

Today you should be able to deal with tasks that demand concentration. Your self-discipline is so good that you can deal with matters you would normally leave alone. At the same time you will discover that experience is definitely the best teacher, which is why you undertake repeated jobs with such efficiency.

16 WEDNESDAY
Moon Age Day 1   Moon Sign Gemini

Making progress at the moment seems to be almost totally dependent on other people, which can be slightly annoying on one level. On the other hand, you get on well with people and their presence in your life is important to you so there are mutual benefits to be had if you reconcile yourself to this.

17 THURSDAY
Moon Age Day 2   Moon Sign Gemini

Your partner might disagree with something you are saying or something you wish to do. Before you get on your high horse about this it might be sensible to look at the situation from their point of view. Perhaps there are underlying issues that you are not aware of, so think carefully before you take independent action.

18 FRIDAY
Moon Age Day 3   Moon Sign Cancer

This is a time when personal gambles are likely to work out well for you. If you have decided on a particular course of action, this is the day to push forward into uncharted but exciting territories. Rely on your own gut feelings and allow your natural talents to emerge. Trends are on your side – but that still means putting in the maximum effort.

19 SATURDAY
Moon Age Day 4   Moon Sign Cancer

Your instincts for making money have rarely been better than they are likely to be today, so you can afford to gamble just a little because you are not really taking chances at all. Getting what you want from life is easier now and there are plenty of people around who simply adore you and who would be willing to give you support.

20 SUNDAY
Moon Age Day 5   Moon Sign Leo

You may be sought out for your advice on a number of different occasions today. That's not too surprising because everyone wants to know what you think. You are straight and level in your dealings with the world and although on occasions you might wish you were not quite so understanding, it really is a gift.

21 MONDAY
Moon Age Day 6   Moon Sign Leo

When it comes to the practical side of life people generally seem to have plenty of goodwill to offer you. What they are really doing is repaying you for all the times you have put yourself out on their behalf. Stand by for something slightly embarrassing but nevertheless positive happening in terms of a personal attachment.

22 TUESDAY
Moon Age Day 7   Moon Sign Leo

Just about everything today conspires to reveal you at your most elegant, particularly in the way you present yourself to the world. You will look and feel smart and might easily choose today to visit the hairdresser or a clothes shop. The way you look can have a great bearing on the way you feel and even act.

23 WEDNESDAY
Moon Age Day 8   Moon Sign Virgo

You could be quite unhappy with superficial answers to the questions you ask today and there is little doubt that you will be turning over stones wherever you go, if only to see what is under them. On the journey you are presently taking through life there are many signposts and your job is to take note of as many of them as you can.

24 THURSDAY
Moon Age Day 9   Moon Sign Virgo

In-depth discussions work well, especially since you are very intuitive just now and have a sense of what people really mean, despite what they might actually be saying. Family relationships are also important at this time and you will be happy to spend time with your loved ones, some of whom may have important things to tell you.

25 FRIDAY   *Moon Age Day 10   Moon Sign Libra*

Someone understands only too well how you feel today and is likely to be sympathetic, both to your point of view and your needs. Listen to some relaxing music today and get carried away on a tide of emotion. Alternatively, you could watch a film that takes you straight back to an earlier time.

26 SATURDAY   *Moon Age Day 11   Moon Sign Libra*

Romantic matters are likely to go smoothly and amiably at this time. There are gains to be made from all relationships, including those which are financial rather than personal. If you are making any purchases today make sure you get value for money and if necessary hold on to your cash until you can get a better deal.

27 SUNDAY   *Moon Age Day 12   Moon Sign Scorpio*

A flexible attitude to business will serve you well today. Perhaps a change of job is in the offing, or you could be thinking about going out on your own in some way. Despite this, partnerships also look good and you can co-operate well, even with people you don't get on with that well as a rule.

28 MONDAY   *Moon Age Day 13   Moon Sign Scorpio*

What is happening in close relationships right now should seem to be quite encouraging. People are easy to deal with and very much inclined to follow your own line of reasoning. This is a day on which you will want to look and feel good, so do all you can to present yourself positively and attractively.

29 TUESDAY   *Moon Age Day 14   Moon Sign Sagittarius*

Your perception and insight enables you to solve tough problems, and in only a fraction of the time it would take other people to sort them out. You actually relish a challenge at this time and won't easily be swayed by judgements you see as being in any way suspect. Your confidence in your ability to start something new and exciting is growing.

30 WEDNESDAY *Moon Age Day 15* *Moon Sign Sagittarius*

You should find that personal, especially romantic, attachments make your life more entertaining and easier to cope with today. You feel warmth and a closeness that is stronger than ever and you may even feel slightly emotional about it. This can be quite a special sort of Wednesday if you allow it to be.

31 THURSDAY *Moon Age Day 16* *Moon Sign Sagittarius*

Great opportunities could emerge around now and you will want to do everything you can to make the most of them. Your finances look stronger and you may be in the market for some sort of deal that will throw up handsome dividends later. Most important of all, you are attracting the most positive sort of attention all day long.

June

2018

1 FRIDAY
Moon Age Day 17   Moon Sign Capricorn

This could be a time when circumstances will block some of your plans, or at the very least make them slightly more difficult to accomplish. The best way to handle the lunar low is to allow time to pass while you take a well-earned break. A few necessary routines shouldn't faze you though.

2 SATURDAY
Moon Age Day 18   Moon Sign Capricorn

If it is harder today to get your message across you can at least be fairly certain that things will change again by tomorrow. Try not to be too restless and settle yourself to something quiet that you enjoy doing. There should be plenty of reassurance from loved ones and the chance to catch up with people in and around your home.

3 SUNDAY
Moon Age Day 19   Moon Sign Aquarius

Some plans may not be quite as well thought out as you had hoped on this Sunday, or perhaps others are finding ways to scupper things for you. The chances are that they are not doing this deliberately, so instead of losing your temper it might be best to laugh it off and start again. Things may turn out even better.

4 MONDAY
Moon Age Day 20   Moon Sign Aquarius

When it comes to professional matters you should now be working hard and making significant ground. You will have a particularly easy way in terms of your relationships with superiors, yet without alienating yourself from colleagues. Once work is over, it's time to have some fun.

5 TUESDAY   *Moon Age Day 21   Moon Sign Aquarius*

Personal freedom is important to you at the best of times but right now it seems to be essential. You won't be happy if you sense you are being restricted in any way and having your wings clipped is not something you would allow under present trends. However, you should be quite willing to share your adventures with others.

6 WEDNESDAY   *Moon Age Day 22   Moon Sign Pisces*

It is possible that you could now experience a few problems coming from the direction of friends. This is not necessarily the best time of the month for co-operation or harmony within groups. Personal ties, however, are a different matter. Romance will be high on your agenda and looks very good indeed.

7 THURSDAY   *Moon Age Day 23   Moon Sign Pisces*

Keep abreast of news and views within your community, but don't get too involved in any of them for the moment. You now need to stand aloof from any local politics or from the desire of those close to you to make changes. By tomorrow you will be much more active and reactive but for the moment you are a closed book.

8 FRIDAY   *Moon Age Day 24   Moon Sign Aries*

Today brings you a great chance to make new decisions and clear choices. You are now at your most practical, so it should not be hard to put your plans into action. With a little ingenuity you can think up ways of doing things that never occurred to you before and at the same time score some successes.

9 SATURDAY   *Moon Age Day 25   Moon Sign Aries*

At work you are now efficient, accommodating and able to make significant headway. Crabs who have been out of work for a while can expect to hear something to their advantage before very long and you should be quite optimistic in a general sense. This makes you good to know, which is why friends gather around you.

10 SUNDAY
Moon Age Day 26   Moon Sign Aries

Most planetary trends now turn your mind in the direction of private emotional issues, which makes you slightly more contemplative and keen to talk things through with your partner. Family members might have been difficult to read over the last few days but the chances are that you can now establish better contact with them.

11 MONDAY
Moon Age Day 27   Moon Sign Taurus

Confidence remains the key, even on those occasions when you don't actually have very much of it. You should be able to hide these feelings from those around you and in doing so, colleagues and friends will be naturally inclined to follow your lead. Double-check details relating to meetings.

12 TUESDAY
Moon Age Day 28   Moon Sign Taurus

Your imagination is strong and there should also be new practical ways to solve problems that could have been dogging you for a while. Today awakens you to previously unknown possibilities and there should be a tinge of excitement about. Get in touch with people who live at a significant distance from you.

13 WEDNESDAY
Moon Age Day 0   Moon Sign Gemini

Avoid unnecessary tension at home by keeping busy away from your usual domestic surroundings. This problem, if it occurs at all, is tied to your present need for freedom and diversity. When you feel you are being restricted by responsibility you may be inclined to react somewhat harshly – or else find ways to change things.

14 THURSDAY
Moon Age Day 1   Moon Sign Gemini

Take a journey and get to see the outside world today. Even if you only have an hour or two to spare you can go somewhere. At the same time you will be thirsty for culture so an art gallery, a museum or somewhere equally stimulating might appeal to you. Try to share your interests with people who are like-minded.

15 FRIDAY
Moon Age Day 2   Moon Sign Cancer

You could be slightly in the dark as far as short-term finances are concerned and if this is indeed the case you will need to do some delving in order to establish what is actually going on. There are some positive gains to be made in terms of romance and you should notice that your general popularity is once again on the increase.

16 SATURDAY
Moon Age Day 3   Moon Sign Cancer

Get on with working towards professional goals if you can – though of course this might not be possible unless you work at the weekend. You still have your planning head on and will be keen to get things moving in every sphere of your life. Restrictions are likely to bore you, which is why you are so adventurous and freewheeling now.

17 SUNDAY
Moon Age Day 4   Moon Sign Leo

There could well be a battle of wills going on at the moment and you will be right in the middle of it. Although you are generally easy-going and willing to fall into line, this is definitely not the case right now. Your attitude might shock someone but it is not a bad thing to shake people up once in a while.

18 MONDAY
Moon Age Day 5   Moon Sign Leo

The time is right to strike and this applies to just about any area of your life. Whilst things will be quieter in a personal sense, you are showing your best side to the world at large. Your capabilities have never been as pronounced as they are right now and others will be only too willing to take your ideas and plans into account.

19 TUESDAY
Moon Age Day 6   Moon Sign Virgo

Your enthusiasm continues unabated, which makes you good to have around. Cancer is a delightful zodiac sign because you are able to complement others while always retaining your own sincerity and integrity. If you have recently started a new and important relationship it should be going from strength to strength.

20 WEDNESDAY *Moon Age Day 7   Moon Sign Virgo*

It looks as though you will have all the support you need today, though with leisure and pleasure more important to you at the moment than advancement, you won't be too keen to get involved in very practical or professional issues. The Crab needs to relax and there are any number of options open to you on this June day.

21 THURSDAY *Moon Age Day 8   Moon Sign Libra*

Now is the right time to move upward and outward. There are many favourable trends in your solar chart leading to a number of potentially successful opportunities. If these are professional in nature these might be best to wait until tomorrow but in the meantime get planning furiously.

22 FRIDAY *Moon Age Day 9   Moon Sign Libra*

Now you can definitely find yourself in the right place to make significant headway and at the same time you will be both cheerful and very persuasive. Don't wait around for things to turn your way because, as the saying goes, 'fortune favours the brave'. If there is something you really want, now is surely the best time to ask for it.

23 SATURDAY *Moon Age Day 10   Moon Sign Scorpio*

There could be a slight emphasis today on personal concerns and probably also on family members, some of whom are behaving in a fairly unusual way. With your usual Crab tact you need to find out what is going on and to do everything you can to put matters right. This should be quite easy to achieve under present trends.

24 SUNDAY *Moon Age Day 11   Moon Sign Scorpio*

Keep up your present search for change and variety. With planetary trends being what they are you can also seek new intellectual experiences. Not everyone around you understands the way your mind is working for the moment but that doesn't matter because you also have what it takes to charm the birds from the trees.

25 MONDAY · Moon Age Day 12 · Moon Sign Scorpio

It's a certain fact that your ideas and opinions will not appeal to everyone at the start of this new working week. This will be especially true in a professional sense. You need to explain yourself very carefully and to give those around you the chance to air their views as well. You can get your own way if you at least appear flexible.

26 TUESDAY · Moon Age Day 13 · Moon Sign Sagittarius

Today should be refreshing and inspirational on the social scene and people who come new to your life at this time could well become deep and abiding friends eventually. When it comes to getting changes underway at home you would be best off looking at original possibilities and will want to find some way to brighten up your house.

27 WEDNESDAY · Moon Age Day 14 · Moon Sign Sagittarius

New people should prove to be quite stimulating, though you also need to bear old friends in mind because although they might seem less than inspiring right now, when the chips are down you can always rely on them. Romance is in the air for some Crabs under present trends and new relationships can turn out to be passionate.

28 THURSDAY · Moon Age Day 15 · Moon Sign Capricorn

In the main what you get out of life today is directly proportional to the amount of effort you put in. Don't be too quick to jump to any conclusions but work steadily towards your objectives, bearing in mind that you only have one pair of hands. A calm and rational approach will bring you more than your fair share of rewards.

29 FRIDAY · Moon Age Day 16 · Moon Sign Capricorn

This is a time during which you will almost certainly capitalise on the opportunity to do something novel or different. The more variety you manage to get into your life the better you are going to feel. Ring the changes all through the day and get some fresh air at some stage. Even a walk in the park would be better than nothing.

30 SATURDAY   *Moon Age Day 17   Moon Sign Capricorn*

Some hopeful or interesting news is likely to be coming your way on a day during which communications of all sorts proves to be especially important. Answer all texts, emails and letters as quickly as possible and also chase up a note or parcel that might have gone astray. Don't be surprised if you find yourself gossiping at the moment.

July

2018

1 SUNDAY
Moon Age Day 18   Moon Sign Aquarius

It's time to make a difference and since you probably won't be working on a Sunday you should turn your attention to socialising and also to improving your personal environment in some way. If the weather is really good you might decide on a barbecue or some other sort of party that gets everyone involved.

2 MONDAY
Moon Age Day 19   Moon Sign Aquarius

You can now get to the heart of a personal matter and you may find yourself involved in deep and meaningful conversations with those to whom you are particularly close. The attitude of some friends might be difficult to understand and a little probing will probably be necessary if you are to discover what is really going on.

3 TUESDAY
Moon Age Day 20   Moon Sign Pisces

Find some way to improve your education or to broaden your knowledge in terms of practical skills. It doesn't matter how old you are because the Crab is constantly learning and is usually happy to do so. Try not to be too available for some family members who may well be taking advantage of your good nature.

4 WEDNESDAY
Moon Age Day 21   Moon Sign Pisces

The emphasis in your personal life shifts from the superficial to the very deep. It is possible that your partner or a close family member wants to take you into their confidence about something that might slightly surprise you. Whatever the revelation may be it would be sensible to try to take it in your stride.

5 THURSDAY
Moon Age Day 22   Moon Sign Pisces

Your social life tends to be the most rewarding area of today and perhaps for the remainder of this week. Success can come from group matters and from being able to rely on the support of many different people. When you are involved in situations with others it is likely that you will be elected as the natural leader.

6 FRIDAY
Moon Age Day 23   Moon Sign Aries

It looks as though you will be very susceptible to the influence of certain people. That's fine, just as long as you know that these individuals are reliable and that they are not somehow trying to fool you. Going for any sort of extreme is not to be recommended right now and a slow and steady pace works best.

7 SATURDAY
Moon Age Day 24   Moon Sign Aries

A slightly more cautious approach will be necessary today and this is especially the case in terms of finances. Take a close look at your budget before you spend lavishly, or perhaps before you spend anything. On the personal front you are likely to be making significant ground when it comes to impressing someone you care for.

8 SUNDAY
Moon Age Day 25   Moon Sign Taurus

Today you will be communicating your ideas in a straightforward and no-nonsense sort of way but this does not mean you will be in any way abrupt. Because you are leaving others in no doubt as to the way you feel about situations there won't be any confusion. Being precise is the surest key towards significant gains at present.

9 MONDAY
Moon Age Day 26   Moon Sign Taurus

Focus now on your social life and also concentrate on letting your romantic partner know just how important they are to you. It looks as though you will be increasingly poetic and sweeping people off their feet is going to be easy. Life should be generally straightforward for the moment.

10 TUESDAY · *Moon Age Day 27 · Moon Sign Gemini*

Now is a good time to re-examine your emotional nature and to address a few issues that may have been buried below the surface. A good heart-to-heart talk with someone you trust may also be in order, so that you can unburden yourself of something that has been bugging you for a while. Once you have spoken out you will feel better.

11 WEDNESDAY · *Moon Age Day 28 · Moon Sign Gemini*

You should tend to be quite relaxed under the present planetary configuration and that means you probably will not be pushing yourself all that hard. The chances are that you are ahead of yourself as far as work and general responsibilities are concerned so you can probably afford to take some time out to do whatever takes your fancy.

12 THURSDAY · *Moon Age Day 29 · Moon Sign Cancer*

Your outlook remains enterprising and you should be just about as cheerful as the Crab gets. This makes you great to have around and is a good sign for today. The lunar high increases your chances of getting what you want materially and with Venus in its present position this is likely to extend to your romantic life too.

13 FRIDAY · *Moon Age Day 0 · Moon Sign Cancer*

Your self-confidence is now likely to be going from strength to strength. There are gains to be made from putting yourself in the best possible position to take up unexpected gains and you will be happy to try as many new possibilities as you can. Friends will be extra helpful, though they are only really responding to your attitude.

14 SATURDAY · *Moon Age Day 1 · Moon Sign Leo*

Consistency seems to be the best key to personal success at this stage of the week and you will probably find that you get yourself into a fix if you jump about from one job to another. A sense of proportion is also necessary but this is going to be more difficult to achieve at a time when excitement seems to be the norm for you.

15 SUNDAY
Moon Age Day 2   Moon Sign Leo

Use your energy to help others in practical ways, even if you know you can't do everything you would wish. Support is on the way for some of your more outrageous schemes and for plans that have been at the back of your mind for weeks or months. Mixing with the right people can be especially important if you work today.

16 MONDAY
Moon Age Day 3   Moon Sign Virgo

It is important to be as organised as possible today and don't allow yourself to be bamboozled into situations that are not of your choosing. Should you find yourself somewhat short of cash at the moment it probably will not be an issue. The most important things in life turn out to be absolutely free of charge.

17 TUESDAY
Moon Age Day 4   Moon Sign Virgo

You can probably expect a rather strange sort of day, but certainly not one that works against your best interests. The odd, the off-beat and the downright weird all have their particular appeal and you may be accused of being somewhat strange yourself! Never mind, you're an original and that's what counts.

18 WEDNESDAY
Moon Age Day 5   Moon Sign Libra

You should not expect to copy anyone else's way of doing things today. Continue to show your originality and to demonstrate just how much you know about life and people. There are some potentially interesting possibilities around when it comes to love and there could be some sort of promotion in store for you.

19 THURSDAY
Moon Age Day 6   Moon Sign Libra

Your desire to communicate with others now increases, along with curiosity. Simple answers won't suffice and you need to know why everything works in the way it does. Look out for some small financial gains that could lead to much more in the longer-term. Even inconsequential remarks by friends can have far-reaching implications.

20 FRIDAY   *Moon Age Day 7   Moon Sign Libra*

Now is the time to cultivate new contacts and to make the most of people you meet, no matter how you come across them. The more unusual or original they may be, the greater is the likelihood you will have something in common with them. You need something today help you avoid a sense of lethargy.

21 SATURDAY   *Moon Age Day 8   Moon Sign Scorpio*

Although there are some ups and downs to deal with right now, in the main life should seem to be going your way. It's vital to concentrate on details otherwise situations may well slip away from you without you realising. In social settings you can now appear at your best, even if you don't think you are.

22 SUNDAY   *Moon Age Day 9   Moon Sign Scorpio*

This ought to be a very advantageous period in terms of your career, though it's possible you can't do anything concrete about it on a Sunday. Even so, you can think and plan, so that by the time the new week starts you will be right on the mark and ready to go. Don't be held back by the negative vibes of others.

23 MONDAY   *Moon Age Day 10   Moon Sign Sagittarius*

This is probably the best time of the month to make the most of a busy and happy social life. It's unlikely you will be short of friends because of your birth sign but if this seems to have been the case recently, don't worry. Times are changing and with just a little effort on your part you will find new associations galore.

24 TUESDAY   *Moon Age Day 11   Moon Sign Sagittarius*

You should persist in seeking out the new and unusual, no matter where you find it in life today. Eccentricity may often grab your attention but rarely more so than right now. There may also be a touch of nostalgia visiting you at the moment. This isn't of much use but it's harmless.

25 WEDNESDAY   *Moon Age Day 12   Moon Sign Capricorn*

You may have some trouble getting all you want out of today because you have the lunar low to contend with. Keep up your efforts all the same because you also have some strong supporting planets and although you might have to put in extra effort you can still win through. Unforced errors are likely so pay attention.

26 THURSDAY   *Moon Age Day 13   Moon Sign Capricorn*

Don't get hung up on punctuality today because delays are now more or less inevitable. As long as you get where you want to be it probably won't matter all that much if you have to reorganise your schedule or rely on others. By the evening you should be back on course as far as your favoured plans are concerned.

27 FRIDAY   *Moon Age Day 14   Moon Sign Capricorn*

Friendships should be a major force in your life as the weekend approaches and you can make the very most out of the attachment you feel for others. In a few cases what started out as a friendship may become something much more but whether or not you are getting romantic, you will appreciate the things those around you do for you.

28 SATURDAY   *Moon Age Day 15   Moon Sign Aquarius*

You now tend to desire more in the way of fun and stimulation that makes you feel truly alive. If that means taking physical chances, you should probably think twice because you could be slightly susceptible to minor injuries at this time. Share your loving and carefree nature with as many people as possible.

29 SUNDAY   *Moon Age Day 16   Moon Sign Aquarius*

You can get the maximum from any outdoor pursuits today and you will be far more inclined to push yourself in a physical sense than is often the case. If there is anything major to be done, get it out of the way today and then allow yourself the time you need to rest and reflect on life.

30 MONDAY
Moon Age Day 17   Moon Sign Pisces

Try to stay on the right side of those who matter at work, even if these are people to whom you are directly responsible. It's likely that junior colleagues can be of help to you and might have some timely advice that you won't want to pass up. Avoid getting socially involved with known trouble-makers.

31 TUESDAY
Moon Age Day 18   Moon Sign Pisces

This period is marked by an increasing association with other people as a result of your career choices and personal decisions. The days ahead are likely to be quite interesting and filled with new experiences. You will be involved with professional colleagues in situations that go well beyond what is expected of you at work.

August

2018

1 WEDNESDAY ☿ *Moon Age Day 19   Moon Sign Pisces*

Your attitude now is ground breaking and innovative. New ideas get the green light and you should be able to inspire other people with the way you get on with things. Present planetary positions mean you are ready to overcome each challenge as it arises, though it might be best to avoid looking for them.

2 THURSDAY ☿ *Moon Age Day 20   Moon Sign Aries*

If things stand still today you could find yourself getting very restless and inclined to jump about from foot to foot. For this reason you will probably prefer to be proactive and to make things happen. Be careful though because you might be inclined to push other people into situations that would not normally be of their own choosing.

3 FRIDAY ☿ *Moon Age Day 21   Moon Sign Aries*

This is a day for inspiration and creativity in equal quantities. Getting things done will not be at all hard and you have what it takes to inspire those around you – which is always a good sign. The only slight potential problem could be a tendency towards fuzzy thinking so it is important to stay focused at all times.

4 SATURDAY ☿ *Moon Age Day 22   Moon Sign Taurus*

People who have merely been acquaintances in the past are now likely to become friends. You want to be on good terms with just about everyone and that means putting yourself out to accommodate different ideas and opinions. Fortunately this is not at all a difficult state of affairs for the Crab at the moment.

121

5 SUNDAY ☿ *Moon Age Day 23 Moon Sign Taurus*

Save time today for celebrating and enjoying yourself. An important personal relationship will be at the forefront of your mind and you will want to make the best possible impression on someone who has been, and remains, central to your thinking. Being a loner is not an option under present trends and you are extremely sociable.

6 MONDAY ☿ *Moon Age Day 24 Moon Sign Gemini*

Communications are at the top of your list of priorities today and it will seem especially important to make the best of impressions on those with whom you work. As far as your home circumstances are concerned you may be more inclined than usual to switch things around and to try out different ways of organising yourself.

7 TUESDAY ☿ *Moon Age Day 25 Moon Sign Gemini*

This is definitely not the best time for concentration and logic. Several planets are conspiring to make you active and reactive, though not quite as deep-thinking as would normally be the case. It is the immediate that grabs you at this time and you respond especially positively to anything that sounds as though it might be exciting.

8 WEDNESDAY ☿ *Moon Age Day 26 Moon Sign Gemini*

You may feel significantly more intuitive than usual and this reflects itself in a number of different ways. Lose yourself in home and family if you can, though if you are committed to being out there in the wider world all day, find little periods when you can relax. Too much concentration will tire you at this time.

9 THURSDAY ☿ *Moon Age Day 27 Moon Sign Cancer*

The best way to approach the world today is head on. The lunar high offers you all the incentives you could possibly need and makes you positively explode with ideas. It looks as though success will follow you throughout the day and new incentives should be coming in all the time.

10 FRIDAY ☿ *Moon Age Day 28   Moon Sign Cancer*

You can now be very skilled at implementing necessary changes to your normal routines and you won't want to sit around and think too much under present trends. On the contrary you will be at your happiest when you are making the running and when others are content to follow your lead.

11 SATURDAY ☿ *Moon Age Day 0   Moon Sign Leo*

Ensuring that you are ready for new plans and revolutionary schemes is very important. It would be better not to embark on anything out of the ordinary unless you have worked out your strategies first because you are not presently quite as good at thinking on your feet as would generally be the case for the Crab.

12 SUNDAY ☿ *Moon Age Day 1   Moon Sign Leo*

The social world might hold less appeal for you now, and instead you focus on your own inner self. What you do for others in a concrete sense remains important but you are likely to want to run the show when you are amongst friends. This is certainly a day for enjoyment but what form it takes remains a mystery.

13 MONDAY ☿ *Moon Age Day 2   Moon Sign Virgo*

Keep in contact with a variety of alternative sorts of people, especially those from different walks of life. Life can be quite rewarding but in an insular mood you can be somewhat difficult for others to fathom. Actually this can be an advantage because the harder you are to read the more attractive you seem to be.

14 TUESDAY ☿ *Moon Age Day 3   Moon Sign Virgo*

Don't look for a means of escape today if you feel threatened in some way. You have what it takes to look demons clear in the face and you can win out, even in situations that might make you nervous. Getting what you want from your partner is easy and it would be simplicity itself to settle for romance and little else at this time.

15 WEDNESDAY ☿   *Moon Age Day 4   Moon Sign Libra*

Conservative ideas are not for you at this time and you can be quite radical in your approach to almost anything. People who are used to your kind and gentle ways might be slightly surprised to see how reactive and assertive you are capable of being. Before the day is out you might even surprise yourself.

16 THURSDAY ☿   *Moon Age Day 5   Moon Sign Libra*

You will enjoy being around other people today and can get a great deal from groups of almost any sort. In a gregarious mood, the Crab certainly won't want to spend too much time on its own at the moment. Just be careful you don't end up cracking jokes that turn out to be somewhat less than appropriate.

17 FRIDAY ☿   *Moon Age Day 6   Moon Sign Scorpio*

It is social trends that really shine out today and you will want to mix as freely as possible with the greatest cross-section of people you can. Happy to compromise, even on those occasions when you cannot accept the plans that colleagues or friends are putting forward you suggest acceptable alternatives.

18 SATURDAY ☿   *Moon Age Day 7   Moon Sign Scorpio*

Right now you have excellent instincts for teamwork and for getting jobs right in conjunction with colleagues. Crabs who work on their own or who are between jobs or retired will need to forge different sorts of alliances at present. You are far from being a solitary creature and definitely need company.

19 SUNDAY   *Moon Age Day 8   Moon Sign Sagittarius*

There are situations around today that will test your patience but fortunately these are likely to be few and far between. What might upset you just a little is being around people who seem to do the wrong thing time and again, no matter how much you advise them to the contrary. Even your tolerance has its limits.

20 MONDAY   *Moon Age Day 9   Moon Sign Sagittarius*

There is much enjoyment to be had from relationships, particularly romantic ones. If the love of your life needs a little pepping up, now is the time to put in extra effort. You could be very surprised by the result and your popularity with your lover is likely to be going off the scale now and for a while.

21 TUESDAY   *Moon Age Day 10   Moon Sign Sagittarius*

Keep a careful focus on objectives and make sure that you are well organised from the very start of today. It's true that now is not the best time of the month for innovations and you act best when you know what is expected of you. This might all make for a slightly lack-lustre sort of Tuesday were it not for the input of some of your friends.

22 WEDNESDAY   *Moon Age Day 11   Moon Sign Capricorn*

Communication may not be all you would wish today and it would be quite easy to get hold of the wrong end of any stick. Where details are concerned it would be sensible to check and check again in order to ensure that something important is not missed. The lunar low generally means a quieter social period.

23 THURSDAY   *Moon Age Day 12   Moon Sign Capricorn*

In your personal life there could be the odd tricky situation to deal with today. You will need to take quick and intelligent action if you are to avoid giving offence where none is really intended. With the lunar low moving out of the way later in the day things should settle down and you won't have to be quite so sensitive all the time.

24 FRIDAY   *Moon Age Day 13   Moon Sign Aquarius*

Any attempt to dominate in relationships is going to be doomed to failure for the moment. This doesn't mean that you have to capitulate entirely and do everything that others suggest you should. All that is really necessary is for you to avoid issues you don't like the look of and to put off decisions for a while.

25 SATURDAY   *Moon Age Day 14   Moon Sign Aquarius*

The past has a great influence over you for a day or two and this can be either a good or a bad thing. Nostalgia for its own sake won't help you at all, but learning from past mistakes can. Attitude is important when you are dealing with people you have found slightly difficult to face on previous occasions.

26 SUNDAY   *Moon Age Day 15   Moon Sign Aquarius*

Now you show yourself to be truly independent and although this might not go down well with everyone, you do need to make up your own mind about almost everything and won't take kindly to being told what you should do. Don't let this lead to arguments because you hate them and they rarely help you in any way.

27 MONDAY   *Moon Age Day 16   Moon Sign Pisces*

Around now you begin to develop an even greater desire to help others all you can. There is nothing particularly unusual about this, except in terms of the degree. You might need to be a little careful because some of the advice and practical assistance you are offering is not wanted and certainly won't be welcomed by everyone.

28 TUESDAY   *Moon Age Day 17   Moon Sign Pisces*

All things considered you are likely to be quite socially shy today and might prefer to spend time on your own or with loved ones, rather than throwing in your lot with party-animals. Your recent joie de vivre will return before very long so for the moment simply revel in the chance to be alone with your thoughts.

29 WEDNESDAY   *Moon Age Day 18   Moon Sign Aries*

At home you show yourself to be a good diplomat and can absorb some of the criticism that might be coming from your partner or family members. You realise that this is not directed specifically at you and have what it takes to pour oil on troubled waters. In most situations now you will be calm and collected.

30 THURSDAY   *Moon Age Day 19   Moon Sign Aries*

Don't let others misunderstand you, even if it means explaining yourself time and again. Positive thinking might not be your forte at present and you will need significant proof before you embark on anything you see as being chancy or potentially hazardous. You will even be sticking to rules for most of today.

31 FRIDAY   *Moon Age Day 20   Moon Sign Aries*

Right now you need great trust, good company and excellent ideas for the future. Keep up a sense of optimism and you can't go far wrong, though there will be moments today when you doubt your own capabilities for a while. One thing is certain, you are well tuned in to what motivates those around you.

September 2018

1 SATURDAY
Moon Age Day 21   Moon Sign Taurus

Don't hesitate to forego your own desires and wishes on account of your hopes for those around you. This is particularly appropriate in terms of your partner and you will go to almost any lengths at the moment for those you care about the most. Not everyone is going to be on your side, especially at work, but those who matter will be.

2 SUNDAY
Moon Age Day 22   Moon Sign Taurus

There is a small chance you will seek a little solitude today but whatever you decide to do you will be contemplative and not inclined to push yourself forward. All people need thinking time and the Crab is no different in this regard. You may be avidly planning your next move at work or in a particular relationship.

3 MONDAY
Moon Age Day 23   Moon Sign Gemini

Short trips taken at this time can be therapeutic and can offer you a different sort of insight into certain issues that could have puzzled you of late. Valuable information is likely to be coming your way at this time and you really need to take notice of all the little messages that life is handing to you. Look for new experiences later in the day.

4 TUESDAY
Moon Age Day 24   Moon Sign Gemini

You may find yourself preoccupied with a personal or emotional matter at some stage today. Try not to dwell on things and draw your present experiences from as large a cross section of life as possible. By turning your attention outwards you may find the answers that evade you when you think too deeply.

5 WEDNESDAY   *Moon Age Day 25   Moon Sign Cancer*

Professional matters are the ones that really stand out as being good during this particular lunar high. However, you should be feeling on top form in terms of your social impulses too, and you will want to associate with as many different people as you can. Routines are for the birds today so avoid them.

6 THURSDAY   *Moon Age Day 26   Moon Sign Cancer*

It shouldn't be hard to express yourself today and you should be able to get others to follow your lead without any difficulty at all. Make sure you get out of the house today and do something different. Your luck is likely to be in so you might opt for a shopping spree in the hope of finding some bargains.

7 FRIDAY   *Moon Age Day 27   Moon Sign Leo*

Now you have a natural ability to express yourself and to handle your emotions in a reasoned and adult way. The same can probably not be said to be the case for some of those closest to you. Certain people won't be dealing with their own disappointments in life at all well and it may be up to you to find some way to sort them out.

8 SATURDAY   *Moon Age Day 28   Moon Sign Leo*

As a rule you tend to be quite influenced by other people and their ideas. This is certainly the case at the moment but you won't simply be taking their schemes on board – rather you will be modifying and improving them. What this does for your personal popularity remains to be seen but life looks fairly secure.

9 SUNDAY   *Moon Age Day 0   Moon Sign Virgo*

Changes happening in your social life may feel good. For example, a good friend might be moving to a different district, or it could seem that you are being somehow excluded from a new group. In the end you will be forced to admit that whatever is taking place around you at the moment really was for the best.

10 MONDAY
Moon Age Day 1   Moon Sign Virgo

This could be an ideal opportunity for a trip or holiday of some sort and though this may come as a surprise you need to react as positively and quickly as you can. A change of scene could release you from some of the tensions you have been feeling in the recent past and might slow your mind down from its present frenetic pace.

11 TUESDAY ·
Moon Age Day 2   Moon Sign Libra

Look out for a positive change as far as your monetary fortunes are concerned. It would be in your interest to focus on investments at this time and to think carefully about ways in which you can make whatever money you have grow. Certain luxury items may now be easier to come by – but do you really need them?

12 WEDNESDAY
Moon Age Day 3   Moon Sign Libra

You are pushing hard towards whatever goals are uppermost in your mind at this time and you have what it takes to keep going when others have fallen by the wayside. Some of your personal ambitions could be at odds with your family concerns but there is always a middle path to follow and Crabs are usually good at finding it.

13 THURSDAY
Moon Age Day 4   Moon Sign Scorpio

If there is any disappointment to be dealt with today you should find you have what it takes to carry on regardless and to get through any problems that do arise. Try to find the time to get in touch with people you don't see too often and be as bold as possible when it comes to stating your rights.

14 FRIDAY
Moon Age Day 5   Moon Sign Scorpio

Your imagination is stimulated best when you are in constant touch with others. Although this is not at all surprising for a Cancerian, your contacts with the world at large are more important than ever right now. Trends also suggest that you have something to crow about as far as your love life is concerned.

15 SATURDAY   *Moon Age Day 6   Moon Sign Scorpio*

When it comes to the emotional side of your life you are now likely to be on top form and showing yourself at your very best. Don't be in the least surprised if romantic overtures come from some quite unexpected directions and avoid creating any jealousy around you by making a special fuss of a really important person.

16 SUNDAY   *Moon Age Day 7   Moon Sign Sagittarius*

Today could have a different feel. You would do well to put personal and domestic issues on hold, whilst you choose to get on with something practical. Weekend working Crabs may have to put in that extra bit of effort right now but the results ought to be more than worthwhile. Keep up your efforts socially.

17 MONDAY   *Moon Age Day 8   Moon Sign Sagittarius*

Although it almost certain that you are getting on well with certain individuals, consider if perhaps you are being taken for a ride. It's important today to stick to those who have known you for a long time. Don't expect to make too many gains at work, or indeed in any practical situation that crops up.

18 TUESDAY   *Moon Age Day 9   Moon Sign Capricorn*

You may now be unable to make solid choices and with the lunar low really having a bearing on your life today and tomorrow it will be necessary to listen to the sound advice that is coming from the direction of your friends and especially your partner. Let others do the running, sit back and, if necessary, supervise.

19 WEDNESDAY   *Moon Age Day 10   Moon Sign Capricorn*

Don't depend on big plans today and use the first part of the day to think things through carefully and slowly. You may not feel inclined to socialise as much as you would on a normal day but you should be happy enough when in the bosom of your family. Household chores that are usually a bind may now seem inviting.

20 THURSDAY   *Moon Age Day 11   Moon Sign Aquarius*

The planets smile on you and a minor but important boost to your love life should be coming along today. Getting on with people is rarely difficult for you but should be especially easy right now. In any project that takes deep thought you won't excel for the moment. A degree of superficiality is part of the present planetary line-up.

21 FRIDAY   *Moon Age Day 12   Moon Sign Aquarius*

Today is likely to be somewhat taxing and concentration is called for. Demands are made on both your time and your energy and not everyone you come across is going help you out. Although you find yourself in the middle of a highly social period, today could be something of an exception.

22 SATURDAY   *Moon Age Day 13   Moon Sign Aquarius*

Look out for irritability amongst those you mix with during the weekend. Fortunately this isn't coming from your direction and, on the contrary, you have what it takes to defuse difficult situations and to make people happy. Get some variety into your life and avoid doing the same old things today or tomorrow.

23 SUNDAY   *Moon Age Day 14   Moon Sign Pisces*

This is a co-operative Sunday and discussions of any sort now go extremely well because you are so good at putting your message across. Get on with things today because the more you achieve at the moment, the greater the amount of time you will have to spend on yourself later. Assistance may come from some interesting directions.

24 MONDAY   *Moon Age Day 15   Moon Sign Pisces*

This is a good period for developing spiritual discipline. You seem to be adopting a more meditative view of life and this can bring its own gains. The material side of life is now less important and you probably won't be able to understand why those around you are constantly acquiring new things. You are also very wise at the moment.

25 TUESDAY
Moon Age Day 16   Moon Sign Aries

If there is a specific project that has been captivating your attention for a few days, now is the time to concentrate on it specifically. You have great powers of discrimination at the moment and an overwhelming desire to get things absolutely right. Romantic input seems likely by the end of the day.

26 WEDNESDAY
Moon Age Day 17   Moon Sign Aries

This ought to be a very enriching time as far as intimate relationships are concerned. Trends are good and you have some strong supporting planets in your solar chart. Personal choices really count and this is not the sort of day on which you will want to follow the rules and dictates of anyone else.

27 THURSDAY
Moon Age Day 18   Moon Sign Aries

It appears that you have little choice but to give way to certain emotions now. Perhaps that is no bad thing because at least it allows others to know where they are. Confidence might seem to be lacking but when it comes to making up your mind you certainly won't be left out in the cold. You are more capable now than you believe.

28 FRIDAY
Moon Age Day 19   Moon Sign Taurus

Don't believe everything you hear today. There are people around who have a vested interest in fooling you and some of them might seem quite sincere. Because you are a naturally trusting sort of individual you could easily fall into a trap, but not if you decide from the very start to keep your wits about you.

29 SATURDAY
Moon Age Day 20   Moon Sign Taurus

Although you won't be the best team player this weekend, in a sense it probably doesn't matter because it looks as though almost everyone will be happy to follow your lead. Certain views, probably expressed by friends, won't accord with your own thinking today and you might have to go it alone if you can't bring them round.

30 SUNDAY   *Moon Age Day 21   Moon Sign Gemini*

You could easily find yourself on the wrong side of a misunderstanding today and you need to make sure that you explain yourself as carefully as possible, no matter what company you are in. It doesn't matter how hard you try, you won't be able to do everything you would wish. A degree of patience is quite necessary now.

October

2018

1 MONDAY
Moon Age Day 22   Moon Sign Gemini

Socialising would be good today but there may be disputes to deal with. This is because you are very sure of your ground at the moment and you won't be happy if people try to bamboozle you in any way. There are ways and means of getting what you want today and simple confrontation is not one of them.

2 TUESDAY
Moon Age Day 23   Moon Sign Cancer

Events now reach a high watermark because in addition to the lunar high you are also subject to a host of supporting influences. Taken together these indicate this to be the best time to make your move, especially at work. Socially speaking, you will be the very centre of attention making this an extremely interesting day.

3 WEDNESDAY
Moon Age Day 24   Moon Sign Cancer

Expect some changes of direction today and be prepared to act at a moment's notice when opportunities come your way. You should be more filled with energy and determination than has been the case for a while. Good luck is around while the lunar high lasts so make the most of it.

4 THURSDAY
Moon Age Day 25   Moon Sign Leo

Some of your ideas may not find favour with others at this time and you will have to work slightly harder than you have done recently if you want to get the best from even personal situations. It could be that those around you are just being awkward but in some situations they may have a point. Try to be as diplomatic as possible.

5 FRIDAY
Moon Age Day 26   Moon Sign Leo

You can now probably expect to make a significant amount of progress in a practical sense, though you may lose out slightly in the personality stakes. It could be difficult to maintain your popularity with some people in the face of actions you know you should take. Compromises are called for so get your thinking cap on.

6 SATURDAY
Moon Age Day 27   Moon Sign Virgo

You could again be at odds today with someone who doesn't have the same opinions as you do, particularly regarding money and the way it should be either spent or saved. Once again you must rely on your natural diplomacy and turn on the charm in order to get what you want. Not all your decisions now will be easy but they should be honest.

7 SUNDAY
Moon Age Day 28   Moon Sign Virgo

This would be a very good time to put your persuasive tongue to work at home and this makes negotiations or discussions a piece of cake during Sunday. Some of your personal targets in life are now standing on firmer ground than they may have done earlier in the year and all that is required is patience and determination.

8 MONDAY
Moon Age Day 29   Moon Sign Virgo

You remain optimistic and confident at the start of a new working week and you can put many of your present plans into words that those around you will fully understand. Telling a tale is sometimes difficult for you but at the moment you are quite poetic and inclined to sugar any pill.

9 TUESDAY
Moon Age Day 0   Moon Sign Libra

You should now be feeling quite secure about life because although the last month has been busy and eventful it might also have been a little precarious in some ways. It looks as though you can now consolidate some of your schemes and it is also possible that there will be more money around than has recently been the case.

10 WEDNESDAY — *Moon Age Day 1   Moon Sign Libra*

Social interactions see you happily on the go and quite willing to join in with group activities. Rather than being out there alone in the lead you now show a greater tendency to share and to attribute any success you do have to your friends. This may be true in part but don't be so modest that you fail to recognise your own efforts.

11 THURSDAY — *Moon Age Day 2   Moon Sign Scorpio*

Whilst finances should be looking a little rosier you could notice that relationships are causing you one or two problems. The closer people are to you the greater is the chance that they will misbehave or act in ways of which you do not approve. Try to shrug off any little frustrations and don't over-react to them.

12 FRIDAY — *Moon Age Day 3   Moon Sign Scorpio*

Groups and friendship generally are well highlighted, indicating this to be a day that sees you prospering from the involvement of others in your daily life. Stay sociable and out there amidst your friends and don't allow yourself too much time to sit and ruminate. Activity is now the best tonic for the blues.

13 SATURDAY — *Moon Age Day 4   Moon Sign Sagittarius*

Today you are inclined to be somewhat rash, which could lead to difficulties further down the line. Try to be circumspect and to think about eventualities before they actually come along. A little caution is important in your love life because if you make bold statements you may be challenged to back them up in some way.

14 SUNDAY — *Moon Age Day 5   Moon Sign Sagittarius*

A break from your normal routine seems to be indicated on this particular day and is all the more likely if you have the free time to do whatever takes your fancy. You won't want to be doing anything alone at the moment because you are about as sociable as even the friendly Crab gets. Whatever you do, take friends along with you.

15 MONDAY *Moon Age Day 6 Moon Sign Capricorn*

There are some inevitable frustrations around while the lunar low pays its monthly visit but these are likely to be fleeting and of no real consequence. Don't take on too much today or tomorrow and to give yourself the time you need to rest and relax. Though this might be hard, it would be advantageous.

16 TUESDAY *Moon Age Day 7 Moon Sign Capricorn*

Make this a lay off period between adventures and seek the comfort of your own hearth and home if you possibly can. You should be getting on especially well with family members at the moment and your love life should also be a source of great joy. There might not be too much amusement about for the moment.

17 WEDNESDAY *Moon Age Day 8 Moon Sign Capricorn*

You tend to be seeing things from the point of view of your family life at the moment and perhaps won't be contributing quite as much as usual out there in the wider world. Real fulfilment presently lies amongst your nearest and dearest but this is likely to be a temporary interlude since outside events demand much more of you by tomorrow.

18 THURSDAY *Moon Age Day 9 Moon Sign Aquarius*

The focus is now predominantly on finance and you should find that you have what it takes to attract money – almost without trying. There is unlikely to be a fortune coming your way but little by little there are gains to be made. Strategies made in order to gain more through your work tend to be sound now.

19 FRIDAY *Moon Age Day 10 Moon Sign Aquarius*

A fairly lucrative period continues and you should be able to draw more money from places that are fairly surprising. You will also have a strong desire for luxury in one form or another and will want to be in surroundings that are comfortable and pleasing to the eye. Little passes you by today, either at work or home.

20 SATURDAY
Moon Age Day 11   Moon Sign Pisces

You may now be inclined to rush in where angels fear to tread and if that means you are doing something that annoys family members, you may be in for a roasting as a result. Bearing in mind how much you hate any sort of fuss or argument, it might still be better to let people do what they want, even if you know they are misguided.

21 SUNDAY
Moon Age Day 12   Moon Sign Pisces

Now you really do need to take life one step at a time because if you rush things you are virtually certain to go wrong. Your thinking processes are slightly clouded, perhaps by sentiment, and you need more time to do practically everything. Seek out a little help because there are many people around who are just bursting to lend a hand.

22 MONDAY
Moon Age Day 13   Moon Sign Pisces

Continue to look out for new chances and opportunities that are coming your way all the time. If you need financial assistance in order to develop your ideas, think up unique ways to get it. Guard against waste or extravagance because you hate both and won't be happy with yourself if you fail to do so.

23 TUESDAY
Moon Age Day 14   Moon Sign Aries

Everyday life keeps you happily on the go and you won't be at all reluctant to push your luck a little when you can see the path ahead clearly. Friends will have a special need of you at present and will rely heavily on your advice and your practical assistance. Putting yourself out for others will be no hardship.

24 WEDNESDAY
Moon Age Day 15   Moon Sign Aries

Don't take things to heart on a personal level because there are remarks being made at the moment that are not directed at you, but to which you might attach yourself. Getting hold of the wrong end of the stick is all too easy under present trends but think very carefully before you over-react.

25 THURSDAY   *Moon Age Day 16   Moon Sign Taurus*

You remain highly sensitive to your working and living environment and to the moods of other people. Back your hunches all the way because your intuition is as strong as it gets. When it comes to talks or negotiations you can work wonders and will be so tuned-in that you can handle several different situations at the same time.

26 FRIDAY   *Moon Age Day 17   Moon Sign Taurus*

Expect some slight setbacks today. They might pass you by unnoticed, but if you do register them it should be easy to address them successfully. Family members can be fractious or difficult to understand and one particular friendship might hit a sticky patch. Just as well that your partner is loving and caring.

27 SATURDAY   *Moon Age Day 18   Moon Sign Gemini*

Life for you now means enjoyment and there isn't anyone or anything that can prevent you from having a good time. You are also likely to be extremely creative at the moment and although there is nothing remotely odd about that you can turn your creativity into cash if you think for a while about skills you already possess.

28 SUNDAY   *Moon Age Day 19   Moon Sign Gemini*

As long as you keep things organised there are not likely to be any setbacks today. Much depends on your ability to keep a sense of proportion regarding issues that really don't need your involvement. The problem is that a slightly nosey streak is crossing the Crab's path today and you just can't avoid interfering.

29 MONDAY   *Moon Age Day 20   Moon Sign Cancer*

You can now capitalise on business and financial investments and could receive unexpected assistance in your efforts to increase your salary. You might receive a surprising gift, though it might be difficult to recognise it as such in the beginning. A sideways look at life perhaps works best for the Crab today.

30 TUESDAY   *Moon Age Day 21   Moon Sign Cancer*

You look and feel strong when going after your objectives but there is just a slight tendency that you could become slightly too confident for your own good. You still need help in some spheres of life and should not turn down the chance of extra support regarding an issue that could be best described as specialised.

31 WEDNESDAY   *Moon Age Day 22   Moon Sign Cancer*

This is a high point for the Crab and a time during which you will demand the attention of the whole world. It might be sensible to start with friends and colleagues, few of whom fail to notice your attractive nature at the moment. You might not feel much like working hard today but you will know how to party.

November
2018

1 THURSDAY
Moon Age Day 23   Moon Sign Leo

Planetary trends now abound with a beneficial focus on finance. You may have the chance to gamble a little but you are unlikely to take the sort of chances that could lead to major difficulties later. Your decisions are likely to be confident and considered and it looks as though others will be very anxious to follow your lead.

2 FRIDAY
Moon Age Day 24   Moon Sign Leo

You should be so dynamic and forceful in your dealings with people generally that some of them may get a shock. It isn't like you to be dominant as you usually get what you want by using your charm. For the moment you will be anxious to cut to the chase in any situation and you won't tolerate what you see as the stupidity of others very well.

3 SATURDAY
Moon Age Day 25   Moon Sign Virgo

Lots of brand new input comes along and your communication skills turn out to be a distinct advantage to you now. Your curiosity knows no bounds and you are willing to go to any lengths to make new discoveries. Some of these might be disquieting but they are also likely to be exciting.

4 SUNDAY
Moon Age Day 26   Moon Sign Virgo

You can now make a strong impact on your surroundings, especially at home. If you have felt slightly uncomfortable with domestic arrangements, now is the time to change them, well ahead of the Christmas period. It could simply be a change in the furniture or else something far more fundamental. Seek other family opinions.

5 MONDAY
Moon Age Day 27   Moon Sign Libra

Today heralds a new and beneficial period, especially when it comes to practical matters. You should be getting on especially well at work and it looks as though you can expect to be considered for advancement or for some sort of honour. This only goes to prove that you have been doing something right over the last few months.

6 TUESDAY
Moon Age Day 28   Moon Sign Libra

You can now afford to be more ambitious and you will have the clout to back up your wishes for the future. In a professional sense you will come as close to being ruthless as the Crab could ever get – but even this is far short of some of the people surrounding you. Nevertheless you will make an impression and you can forge a new path.

7 WEDNESDAY
Moon Age Day 0   Moon Sign Scorpio

Something you say today is likely to clash with the opinions of people you normally get on with extremely well. The situation cannot be altered but you can realise that people don't always see eye-to-eye and leave it at that. Constantly analysing why individuals say what they do is going to be a real waste of time at the moment.

8 THURSDAY
Moon Age Day 1   Moon Sign Scorpio

You can now be at your intellectual best with sharp insight and an instinctive understanding of how to behave under any given circumstance. Don't expect everyone around you to be equally helpful and try not to be short with people who fail to match your expectations. The Crab's normal patience is sadly missing at present.

9 FRIDAY
Moon Age Day 2   Moon Sign Sagittarius

Quick answers, a great wit and a sense of humour that knows no bounds – all these are gifts that should be evident and even obvious under present trends. You can be quite cutting on occasions and even sarcastic if people cross you. Nobody can doubt that you have an edge and that means people are looking in your direction.

143

10 SATURDAY *Moon Age Day 3   Moon Sign Sagittarius*

Involvement with groups is important at this time and you will get on much better with people en masse than you are likely to do with specific individuals. Almost everyone you meet at the moment will have something interesting to tell you and some of the things you learn could be of practical use later on.

11 SUNDAY *Moon Age Day 4   Moon Sign Sagittarius*

Try as hard as you can to make people understand what you are trying to tell them because the importance of what you are saying is likely to be lost in the complications of life. Even if you have to reinforce your views time and again it will be worth it to get the message across.

12 MONDAY *Moon Age Day 5   Moon Sign Capricorn*

All of a sudden things are likely to slow to a snail's pace, at least as far as your professional and practical life is concerned. The lunar low can bring you to a virtual standstill but it does nothing to shake your resolve. Instead of actually doing things today and tomorrow, plan your next moves.

13 TUESDAY *Moon Age Day 6   Moon Sign Capricorn*

Put major issues and decisions on the back-burner and enjoy watching what is happening around you. It is impossible for you to take part in everything, even though you feel as if you should be doing just that. In matters of the heart you prove to be gentle, understanding and quite willing to listen to an alternative point of view.

14 WEDNESDAY *Moon Age Day 7   Moon Sign Aquarius*

Test out ideas with regard to their ultimate feasibility before you get yourself too deeply involved in them. Many inventive solutions to old problems are now likely to occur to you and your mind is both ingenious and practical. Not everyone seems to like you at the moment but the people who matter the most certainly will.

15 THURSDAY   *Moon Age Day 8   Moon Sign Aquarius*

You are now extremely powerful when it comes to putting across your point of view but people don't really seem to mind as long as you are fair and open-minded. When you could come unstuck is on those occasions when you dominate conversations or show how dismissive you can be regarding a plan of action that isn't your own.

16 FRIDAY   *Moon Age Day 9   Moon Sign Aquarius*

You are now at your best when you are surrounded by your favourite people, though you may not have that much time for those you don't care for. As a general rule you can cover up your animosity but to do so is more difficult at present. Life is all about attitude and yours can be just a little suspect under present planetary trends.

17 SATURDAY   ☿   *Moon Age Day 10   Moon Sign Pisces*

Your reactions at this time are like lightning and you should be quite happy to put yourself at the forefront of events. Any shyness that might have been present a week or two ago has now disappeared and you have a great sense of purpose and perseverance. Delays early in the day can be quickly overcome.

18 SUNDAY   ☿   *Moon Age Day 11   Moon Sign Pisces*

Not everything you assume to be true turns out to be so and there is a short interlude today that allows you to re-think your strategies and to look at things in a different light. This is a time to back your own hunches, even when others say you are wrong. With perseverance you can easily prove a point today.

19 MONDAY   ☿   *Moon Age Day 12   Moon Sign Aries*

Due to increased enthusiasm you remain energetic, active and willing to take on more and more in the way of responsibility. People you don't see very often might return to your life now and you could also be in touch with someone who lives far away. Routines are boring at present so do something about them.

20 TUESDAY ☿ *Moon Age Day 13 Moon Sign Aries*

There is some self-deception around at this time and you need to take special care to check things before you proceed in any new direction. There are people who want to be of assistance to you but do they really know what they are doing? In the end you are better off choosing for yourself and staying self-reliant.

21 WEDNESDAY ☿ *Moon Age Day 14 Moon Sign Taurus*

You are enterprising in your outlook and you won't find it difficult to change direction at a moment's notice. This would be a good time to improve yourself in some way – perhaps taking up a new hobby or beginning to study a new subject. The Crab is on a roll and there's no doubting the fact.

22 THURSDAY ☿ *Moon Age Day 15 Moon Sign Taurus*

An influence comes along right now that is inclined to bring more money into your life. This probably will not come all at once and there won't be any fanfare, but there isn't much doubt that you will be better off in some way soon. Friends prove to be loyal and supportive; on occasions possibly a little too much so.

23 FRIDAY ☿ *Moon Age Day 16 Moon Sign Taurus*

It could seem difficult to retain control over every single aspect of your life, but do you really need to do so? If you allow other people to do what they think is right for you, you could be quite surprised at the result. Creature comforts could seem more inviting than they have been recently but perhaps this is due to the onset of winter.

24 SATURDAY ☿ *Moon Age Day 17 Moon Sign Gemini*

With so much forward-looking optimism about, today ought to be something of a dream. There is no doubting your sociable qualities, the planets at the moment see to that, and you are especially entertaining to have around in any social setting. You could be finding new ways to help those who are less well off than you.

25 SUNDAY ☿ *Moon Age Day 18   Moon Sign Gemini*

Your love life is now positively highlighted and this could be the best time of the month for close attachments. You can also enjoy a renaissance in any creative pursuit and everything you do looks both beautiful and seems wise. People generally are crowding in to get your advice because you are such a fair and open individual.

26 MONDAY ☿ *Moon Age Day 19   Moon Sign Cancer*

This is a good time for general progress and a period during which you will be showing yourself off to the best of your ability. You will be very aware of the way you look and the impression you give to others will also be of supreme importance. General good luck and cheer follows you around.

27 TUESDAY ☿ *Moon Age Day 20   Moon Sign Cancer*

The high-energy phase continues as the lunar high works its magic around you. It seems to make others more amenable to your viewpoints, although what is really happening is that you are charming them into accepting your point of view. Romance also looks good and you are likely to be number one in the estimation of someone important.

28 WEDNESDAY ☿ *Moon Age Day 21   Moon Sign Leo*

You can get on well with everyone today – though there's nothing remotely remarkable about that for the average Cancerian. Your confidence remains generally high and your love life in particular should be looking good. You might decide to take a little risk with regard to a particular venture, but proceed with caution as always.

29 THURSDAY ☿ *Moon Age Day 22   Moon Sign Leo*

Don't be at all surprised if there is an element of confusion around today. It isn't that you fail to realise what you should be doing, it's just that things go wrong in more than one way. All of this should be more of a cause for amusement than annoyance, especially as you are in such a happy and positive frame of mind.

30 FRIDAY ☿ *Moon Age Day 23 Moon Sign Virgo*

Certain social acquaintances may prove to be highly useful to your overall path through life at this time. People who you were not particularly close to even a few weeks ago are now playing a much more important part in your life. Keep your eyes and ears open for new input today, no matter what you happen to be doing.

December
2018

1 SATURDAY ☿ *Moon Age Day 24 Moon Sign Virgo*

As you become ever more resourceful, you start to realise that December could well be the month during which you succeed beyond your previous expectations. A little self-belief is critical to the Crab and you seem to have plenty of it right now. Your creative potential remains good and you know how to make things look beautiful.

2 SUNDAY ☿ *Moon Age Day 25 Moon Sign Libra*

This ought to be a day of great inspiration. You really do have a lot going for you at present and there are gains to be made in several different areas of your life. As far as meetings and agreements are concerned today should prove to be inspirational and the only thing you may have to watch out for is the odd awkward friend.

3 MONDAY ☿ *Moon Age Day 26 Moon Sign Libra*

Making an impact on people who are in a position to do you some good has surely never been easier than it is right now. It's time to strike while the iron is hot and to make your feelings known right across the spectrum of your life. People actively want to hear what you have to say and will react positively.

4 TUESDAY ☿ *Moon Age Day 27 Moon Sign Scorpio*

Someone is likely to be relying on your opinions today – in fact a whole variety of people are apt to do so. It might be something as simple as advice about what to buy at the shops or else an issue that is far more serious but whatever you are called upon to comment on today will be important to somebody, so be totally honest.

5 WEDNESDAY ☿ *Moon Age Day 28* *Moon Sign Scorpio*

If you adopt a critical attitude at home, you are in danger of offering unintentional offence. As a rule you tread very carefully around other people's sensibilities but today's trends make you not quite as understanding as would usually be the case. Bite your tongue before you react harshly right now.

6 THURSDAY ☿ *Moon Age Day 29* *Moon Sign Scorpio*

You might decide to do something completely different today and you are likely to have the support of friends who are as bored by convention as you are. Socially speaking you are on top form and the lure of the Christmas season is now fully upon you. Duties will be far less inviting than adventures at this stage.

7 FRIDAY *Moon Age Day 0* *Moon Sign Sagittarius*

Now it pays great dividends to know what your competitors are up to. If you want to get ahead you will need to make it plain what you want from life. Once you have laid your cards on the table you can afford to be slightly more aggressive in going for the prizes that seem to be on offer.

8 SATURDAY *Moon Age Day 1* *Moon Sign Sagittarius*

You may find yourself involved in a domestic situation that amounts to a clash of wills but as the saying goes there is more than one way to skin a cat. Use your present very positive communication skills to address tricky issues and persuade others to behave appropriately.

9 SUNDAY *Moon Age Day 2* *Moon Sign Capricorn*

Your energy and vitality are now lower than usual and the lunar low takes the wind from your sails when it comes to practical progress. You may have to be content with half measures or else leave some jobs until later. Making excuses won't please you but in some situations there is very little choice but to do so.

10 MONDAY   *Moon Age Day 3   Moon Sign Capricorn*

Your power is limited and it will be necessary to call upon the good offices of friends and colleagues. There is no shame in this and people will be glad to lend you a hand – particularly bearing in mind how much you do for others. Despite a few attendant problems today you are likely to remain essentially optimistic.

11 TUESDAY   *Moon Age Day 4   Moon Sign Aquarius*

At home it will be better to offer support today than to expect it to be coming your way. People might mean to be helpful but what actually happens is that they make a few small problems worse. You remain very dependable and your nearest and dearest will recognise this. Accept that there might not be much time to spend on yourself.

12 WEDNESDAY   *Moon Age Day 5   Moon Sign Aquarius*

Leave some space for the emotions of those around you. Although you might think you feel strongly about certain issues there are other people who are far more emotionally stretched than you. Your caring and understanding nature is a great part of your personality and this really does need to show today.

13 THURSDAY   *Moon Age Day 6   Moon Sign Aquarius*

A more enriched period now makes itself felt. It won't be what happens on the surface that is most interesting at the moment but rather the undertones of life. Almost every person you meet feels they are an expert in one thing or another and this fact alone means you might have to sort out a number of tortured issues.

14 FRIDAY   *Moon Age Day 7   Moon Sign Pisces*

It should now quite easy to express your emotions. This is a good time to clear the air and to say something that has been on your mind for quite a while. As December grows older and the winter weather makes itself known, you could easily be inclined to seek out a warm fireside and the company of family members.

15 SATURDAY
Moon Age Day 8   Moon Sign Pisces

This can be a period of improved relationships and communication with friends. This weekend you will happily sail forth and look for new situations and different kinds of mental stimulation. Your attitude becomes more expansive and you begin to wake up to some exciting new possibilities tied to the season.

16 SUNDAY
Moon Age Day 9   Moon Sign Pisces

Your domestic affairs enter a more expansive phase at this time. It could be that you are making changes ahead of Christmas or simply looking for of a new way of living your life. The changes probably won't be radical but they do count and should help you to feel better about the time of year and more content with your lot.

17 MONDAY
Moon Age Day 10   Moon Sign Aries

Dealings with some other people might seem fairly unsatisfactory, mainly because you can't get them to do exactly what you would wish. There is also a good deal of uncertainty in your mind under present trends and a tendency to do things time and again, even though you know in your heart they were fine before.

18 TUESDAY
Moon Age Day 11   Moon Sign Aries

Activities today tend to be more fun than serious and any truly honest assessment of your life at this time should show you to be generally content with your lot. Of course there are always things you want that you don't have but many of these will come in good time. Don't get too tied to pointless routines today.

19 WEDNESDAY
Moon Age Day 12   Moon Sign Taurus

This would be a very good time to benefit from the diversity of interests that are so typical of your nature under present trends. With more energy at your disposal and the chance to put it to good use, you will find yourself tackling all manner of new jobs. People turn to you for help and advice at the moment, which you are pleased and qualified to offer.

20 THURSDAY
Moon Age Day 13   Moon Sign Taurus

Take things steadily and don't overestimate your capacity for work today. Although you have plenty of energy throughout the month, this may not be specifically the case today. Pace yourself and allow others to take some of the strain. If you go to bed tonight feeling absolutely drained, you may still feel fatigued tomorrow.

21 FRIDAY
Moon Age Day 14   Moon Sign Gemini

This is a day that could be marked by a distinct lack of discipline in practical affairs. In some ways you prefer to let things ride, rather than pitching in and sorting them out once and for all. Your attitudes could be slightly unrealistic and you may need to talk to someone who has more age or experience than you.

22 SATURDAY
Moon Age Day 15   Moon Sign Gemini

If you are slightly quieter today you can be fairly sure that this is a very temporary state of affairs, brought about by the position of the Moon. It's true you will be thinking things through carefully and you may not be quite as gregarious as you have been recently. All of this changes tomorrow when you throw caution to the wind.

23 SUNDAY
Moon Age Day 16   Moon Sign Cancer

The Moon moves into Cancer and that means you will have the lunar high coming along at the very end of the year. Social impulses are as strong as ever and you should have sufficient energy to move around freely and to involve yourself fully in life. Make the most of this.

24 MONDAY
Moon Age Day 17   Moon Sign Cancer

Important changes you want to make at home now become more of a reality and you are definitely in a good position to influence the thinking of people who can be quite intransigent on occasions. Good fortune is on your side and makes for a potentially good and fulfilling Christmas Eve.

25 TUESDAY
Moon Age Day 18   Moon Sign Leo

Christmas Day for Cancer should be great and you may enjoy fruitful encounters with a number of different people today, some of whom are offering the sort of information that is both timely and useful. Where love and romance are concerned, it is not difficult to find the right words to sweep someone off their feet during the festivities.

26 WEDNESDAY
Moon Age Day 19   Moon Sign Leo

It appears that personal and intimate matters bring out the best in you for Boxing Day. Concentrating on the family, rather than distant friends or even work, certainly seems to appeal. If you find yourself facing a mountain of tasks, the best approach is to break them down into easily manageable units and do them one at a time.

27 THURSDAY
Moon Age Day 20   Moon Sign Virgo

There's no doubt about it. You have plenty of new ideas today, even if actually putting them into practice isn't all that easy, what with the holiday period and the necessities of the season. Nevertheless, there is nothing to prevent you from looking at future strategies, and playing one or two of them through in your mind.

28 FRIDAY
Moon Age Day 21   Moon Sign Virgo

Today should find you on top form and eager for almost anything that comes along. It's true that you won't be good at working, but the holiday season is in full swing and the Crab loves to have fun. Some family members may be feeling suitably nostalgic now and you are no exception.

29 SATURDAY
Moon Age Day 22   Moon Sign Libra

Perhaps you feel slightly restricted because you need to mix with as many different sorts of people today as proves to be possible. At the back of your mind are a number of different ideas, some of which involve innovation. There are individuals appearing now who will listen to what you have to say and who may even offer to help.

30 SUNDAY   *Moon Age Day 23   Moon Sign Libra*

Keep your ears open because what you learn in group situations today could prove to be extremely useful in the end. Listen to what is being said but don't commit yourself to joining in unless you are very sure of your ground. You are likely to be awash with energy today and quite willing to take on more than is probably good for you.

31 MONDAY   *Moon Age Day 24   Moon Sign Libra*

You might enter the last day of the year with a little extra seriousness, though not for long. Of course you will want to work out what you have and have not achieved across the last twelve months and also to plan ahead. However, most of what today should be about is enjoying yourself and making things great for everyone around you.

RISING SIGNS FOR CANCER

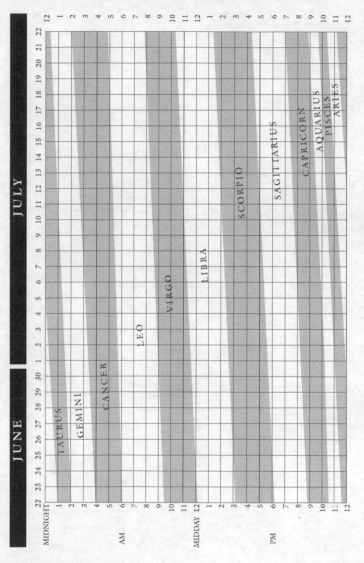

THE ZODIAC, PLANETS AND CORRESPONDENCES

The Earth revolves around the Sun once every calendar year, so when viewed from Earth the Sun appears in a different part of the sky as the year progresses. In astrology, these parts of the sky are divided into the signs of the zodiac and this means that the signs are organised in a circle. The circle begins with Aries and ends with Pisces.

Taking the zodiac sign as a starting point, astrologers then work with all the positions of planets, stars and many other factors to calculate horoscopes and birth charts and tell us what the stars have in store for us.

The table below shows the planets and Elements for each of the signs of the zodiac. Each sign belongs to one of the four Elements: Fire, Air, Earth or Water. Fire signs are creative and enthusiastic; Air signs are mentally active and thoughtful; Earth signs are constructive and practical; Water signs are emotional and have strong feelings.

It also shows the metals and gemstones associated with, or corresponding with, each sign. The correspondence is made when a metal or stone possesses properties that are held in common with a particular sign of the zodiac.

Finally, the table shows the opposite of each star sign – this is the opposite sign in the astrological circle.

Placed	Sign	Symbol	Element	Planet	Metal	Stone	Opposite
1	Aries	Ram	Fire	Mars	Iron	Bloodstone	Libra
2	Taurus	Bull	Earth	Venus	Copper	Sapphire	Scorpio
3	Gemini	Twins	Air	Mercury	Mercury	Tiger's Eye	Sagittarius
4	Cancer	Crab	Water	Moon	Silver	Pearl	Capricorn
5	Leo	Lion	Fire	Sun	Gold	Ruby	Aquarius
6	Virgo	Maiden	Earth	Mercury	Mercury	Sardonyx	Pisces
7	Libra	Scales	Air	Venus	Copper	Sapphire	Aries
8	Scorpio	Scorpion	Water	Pluto	Plutonium	Jasper	Taurus
9	Sagittarius	Archer	Fire	Jupiter	Tin	Topaz	Gemini
10	Capricorn	Goat	Earth	Saturn	Lead	Black Onyx	Cancer
11	Aquarius	Waterbearer	Air	Uranus	Uranium	Amethyst	Leo
12	Pisces	Fishes	Water	Neptune	Tin	Moonstone	Virgo